Wreck Diving

DISCLAIMER:

The information contained in the SSI training materials is intended to give an individual enrolled in a training course a broad perspective of the diving activity. There are many recommendations and suggestions regarding the use of standard and specialized equipment for the activity. Not all of the equipment discussed in the training material can, or will, be used in this activity. The choice of equipment and techniques used in the course is determined by the location of the activity, the environmental conditions and other factors.

A choice of equipment and techniques cannot be made until the dive site is surveyed immediately prior to the dive. Based on the dive site, the decision should be made regarding which equipment and techniques shall be used. The decision belongs to the dive leader and the individual enrolled in the training course.

The intent of all SSI training materials is to give individuals as much information as possible in order for individuals to make their own decisions regarding the diving activity, what equipment should be used and what specific techniques may be needed. The ultimate decision on when and how to dive is for the individual diver to make.

ISBN-13: 978-1-59750-185-9

First Edition
First Printing, 1/95
Second Printing, 4/97

Second Edition
First Printing, 5/07
Second Printing 5/10

PRINTED IN THE USA

This manual is printed using Low-VOC ink.

www.diveSSI.com

Contents

Section 5: Advanced Wreck Diving

Appendix

Acknowledgements

Editor in Chief	Doug McNeese
Manager of Development	Suzanne Fletcher
Author	Daniel Berg
Graphic Designers	Lori Evans, Jennifer Silos
Cover Photos	SSI Staff
Photographers	SSI Staff Daniel Berg, Greg Ochoki
Contributing Photographers	Martin Denison, Black Durgeon, Keith Ibsen, Paolo Lilla, Rick Murchison, Randy Pfizenmaier, SSI Australia, Amy Young
Contributing Editors	Watson DeVore, Doug McNeese, Sheli Smith, Ph.D.
Technical Editors	Thomas Bofferding, Bruce Jameson, Mike Kohut, Stephen Riordan, Paul Rosman

Preface

You will see that each section includes several unique icons to highlight information or add information that relates to the text near it. In some cases, these icons point out information directly associated with the section objectives, while in other cases, the icon indicates a continuing education opportunity. While these icons are designed to help you learn and retain information, they also provide you with an easy reference to important information as you study.

Pearl

"Pearl" the oyster (originally named "Hey!"), is found throughout the text to point out information that we believe is key to a new diver's success. The "pearls of wisdom" that our oyster friend highlights are designed to help you meet section objectives, assist in answering study guide questions and may be used in group discussions with your instructor.

Continuing Education

At Scuba Schools International, we believe that one of the keys to achieving and maintaining success as a diver is taking the "next step" via continuing education. To reinforce that belief, we have put a Continuing Education icon next to topics that correspond to continuing education opportunities available to you through your SSI Dealer. Your SSI Instructor or Dealer will be happy to answer any questions you may have about the continuing education courses listed throughout this manual.

Environment

SSI has always supported and promoted environmental awareness and believes that care for the environment should be a standard part of diver education from start to finish. For these reasons, an environmental icon has been included to highlight important environmental issues as they relate to divers and the underwater world. Topics that you will find the environmental icon next to include the importance of buoyancy control, reef appreciation and conservation, and using your equipment in an environmentally friendly way.

International Use

To meet international English language recommendations, some of the words you come across in this manual may look misspelled. The following is a list of these words in American English and their International counterparts.

American English	International Counterpart
Center	Centre
Meter	Metre
Gray	Grey
Aluminum	Aluminium

Throughout the manual, imperial measurements are listed first followed by the metric conversion. The following conversion units were used to convert the various measurements:

Conversions

1 ATA (Atmospheres Absolute) = 14.7 psi (pounds per square inch)

1 ATA = 1 bar

1 Metre = 3.28 feet

C°= (F° -32) ÷ 1.8

1 kg (kilogram) = 2.2 lbs (pounds)

1 km (kilometre) = .621 miles

Imperial

1 ATA = 33 fsw (feet of sea water)

1 ATA = 34 ffw (feet of fresh water)

Metric

1 BAR = 10 metres of sea water

1 BAR = 10.30 metres of fresh water

Note: For greater ease, many of the conversions in this text have been rounded to the nearest whole number, and may not reflect the exact conversion.

Be Ready for Your Journey

Welcome

Wreck Diving offers a new outlet for adventure and helps satisfy your natural curiosity by providing a glimpse of the past. This program will give you in-depth information on selecting wreck sites, understanding the equipment involved in diving wrecks and how to safely explore wrecks.

Be Ready for Your Journey

All specialty courses are based on our signature training method — the SSI Diver Diamond. To become a comfortable and confident diver, it takes 4 ingredients:

Proper Knowledge

As in all SSI training programs, knowledge is power and replaces fears and fantasies with correct information. In this program, you will acquire the specific knowledge related to the Wreck Diving Specialty.

Proper Skills

Repetition is the mother of all skills. Under the guidance of your SSI Dive Professional, you will learn the specific skills and techniques necessary to properly execute a recreational wreck dive.

Proper Equipment

The safest way to dive is in your won personally fitted Total Diving System. For this and all SSI Continuing Education programs, you may need additional equipment to perform successful wreck dives.

Proper Experience

Gaining the knowledge, skills and equipment to make advanced dives is only one part of the journey. Going diving is the only way you can gain the actual experience needed to become comfortable and confident with your newly learned wreck diving skills.

How Far Do You Want to Go?

If you believe the journey is just as important as the destination, then SSI's Continuing Education is for you. Taking specialties is a great way to hone your skills and learn some new ones. Continuing Education is exciting and limitless. It is your chance to begin exploring beyond the surface. Choose your personal combination of training and diving experience to reach your diving goals today!

SSI's Continuing Education programs are all menu-based home study programs. These specialty programs are designed so that you can learn at your own pace when it's convenient for you. Menu-based means you can take programs in a combined manner or one at a time based on your personal interest. Simply choose from specialties like, Digital Photography, Enriched Air Nitrox, Wreck, Navigation, Boat, or Deep and you're on your way.

Getting involved is easy! If you're not sure which specialties you want to try, sign up for the Advanced Adventurer program. You will be able to take 5 dives and try 5 different specialties. Upon completion you will be recognized with an Advanced Adventurer card. These dives also count towards your rating if you choose to continue your training in one of the specialty areas covered.

For detailed information regarding SSI Specialty programs ask your SSI Dive Center or visit www.diveSSI.com.

Intro

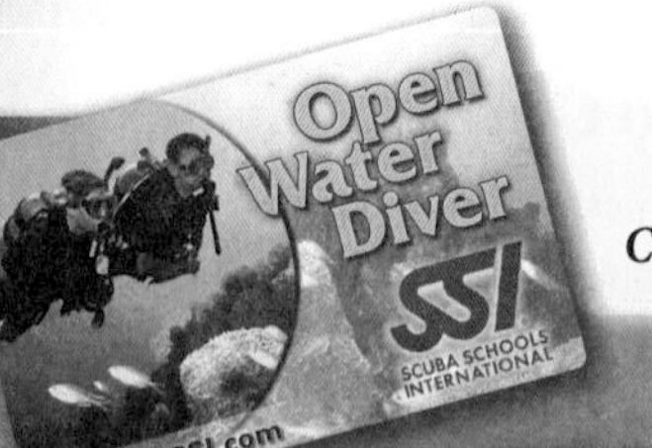

5 OR MORE LOGGED DIVES

LEVEL OF EXPERIENCE: 1

Complete the SSI Open Water Diver course & get this card!

12 OR MORE LOGGED DIVES

LEVEL OF EXPERIENCE: 2

Complete Level 2 dives & 2 Specialty Courses.

24 OR MORE LOGGED DIVES

LEVEL OF EXPERIENCE: 3

Complete Level 3 dives & 4 Specialty Courses.

50 OR MORE LOGGED DIVES

LEVEL OF EXPERIENCE: 4

Complete Level 4 dives, 4 Specialty Courses & the Diver Stress & Rescue Course.

AVAILABLE SPECIALTIES — *Take one or take them all!*

- Adaptive Scuba Diving
- Boat Diving
- Computer Diving
- Deep Diving
- Digital Underwater Photography
- Diver Stress & Rescue
- Dry Suit Diving
- Emergency Training
  - First Aid & CPR
  - Emergency Oxygen
  - AED
- Enriched Air Nitrox
- Equipment Techniques
- Navigation
- Night and Limited Visibility Diving
- Perfect Buoyancy
- Science of Diving
- Search & Recovery
- Technical Extended Range
  - Advanced Nitrox
  - Technical Foundations
  - Decompression Procedures
  - Advanced Decompression
  - Normoxic Trimix
- Waves, Tides & Currents
- Wreck Diving

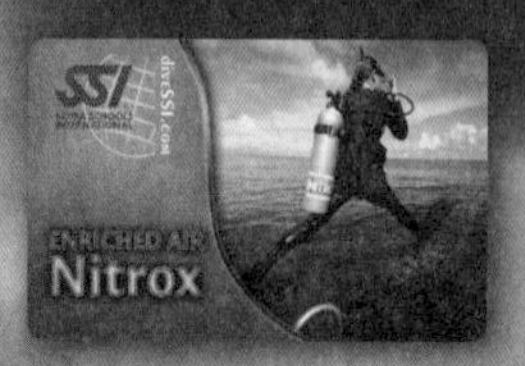

You can become a Dive Professional once you have completed Level 4!
Ask your SSI Dive Center for complete details.

Instructor Levels

Quality Divers Start with Qualified Instructors

SCUBA SCHOOLS INTERNATIONAL DIVE GUIDE

↓

SCUBA SCHOOLS INTERNATIONAL DIVEMASTER

↓

SCUBA SCHOOLS INTERNATIONAL DIVE CONTROL SPECIALIST

↓

SCUBA SCHOOLS INTERNATIONAL OPEN WATER INSTRUCTOR

↓

SCUBA SCHOOLS INTERNATIONAL ADVANCED OPEN WATER INSTRUCTOR

↓

SCUBA SCHOOLS INTERNATIONAL DIVE CONTROL SPECIALIST INSTRUCTOR

↓

SCUBA SCHOOLS INTERNATIONAL INSTRUCTOR TRAINER

Other Instructor Programs

- Specialty Instructor
- Diver Stress & Rescue Instructor
- Enriched Air Nitrox Instructor
- Scuba Rangers Instructor
- Technical Extended Range
  - Advanced Nitrox Instructor
  - Technical Foundations Instructor
  - Decompression Procedures Instructor
  - Advanced Decompression Procedures Instructor
  - Normoxic Trimix Instructor
  - TechXR Instructor Trainer

REWARDS FOR EXPERIENCE

No Training Required!

Taking a specific number of specialties and continuing your pursuit of dives allows you to earn higher rating levels. SSI Ratings are the only ratings in the industry that combine training and experience requirements, proving that SSI Ratings are truly earned.

Reward yourself as you reach new milestones in your diving adventures!

About SSI

Scuba Schools International grew out of the passion of a few avid divers who were intent on making it possible for anyone to learn to scuba dive.

SSI provides education materials, dive training and scuba certification for divers, dive instructors, dive centers and dive resorts around the world. Since 1970, SSI has expanded to 27 International Offices, doing business in 110 countries with training materials in 25 languages representing over 2,400 dive centers and resorts. SSI Certification Cards are welcomed all over the planet, wherever you choose to dive.

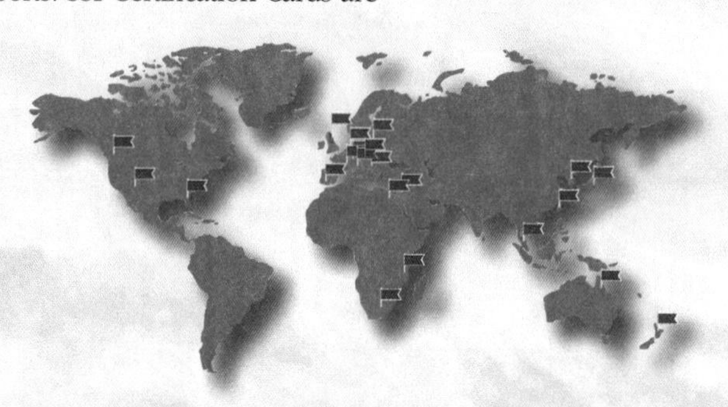

Scuba Schools International is clearly a name you can trust in the diving community and we attribute that success to uncompromising standards and a focus on quality not quantity.

Involvement

As well as being an industry leader, SSI is also a founding member of the industry's standards body in the USA and abroad – in the USA, it's the RSTC (Recreational Scuba Training Council) and in Europe, it's the WRSTC and the EU (European Standards – EN 14153-1-3 for divers and 144413-1-2 for scuba instructors).

Reward Yourself. You Deserve it

Becoming certified in Wreck Diving is an achievement. Be sure to reward yourself for reaching this major milestone with an SSI Wreck Diving certification card. This is an opportunity to commemorate your hard – earned accomplishment.

Where to Go From Here

We are certain that your journey through Wreck will be everything you imagined and more. Don't forget you can always combine other specialties to increase your diving knowledge — the possibilities are limitless. Now let's go have some fun!

Selecting a Wreck Site

1

1

Section 1 Objectives

After completing this section you will be able to:

- Understand the three categories of wrecks,
- Describe various shipwreck laws and the types of protection in place for shipwrecks,
- Understand how to research a shipwreck,
- Describe the various sources for information on shipwrecks.

Wreck diving is a specialized area of scuba diving that can be enjoyed by all diver's, in all areas of the world. It offers the diver a new outlet for adventure, a change from the coral reefs and kelp forests. Wrecks also help satisfy the divers natural curiosity by allowing a glimpse at our past. Each wreck is a time capsule into history waiting to be explored. Within the pages of this book, you will find many helpful hints to start you on your way to becoming a wreck diver. Until now these tricks of the trade were learned through years of experience. Realize that no book can instantly make anyone an expert wreck diver. Our goal is to provide you with needed information and give you a solid foundation upon which to build.

The variability in the type of wrecks and the clarity and condition of the water is what divers need to understand before descending upon an unknown adventure. This program is designed to help the wreck diver gain an understanding of how to judge wreck sites in order to decide the level of skill and equipment that is required to make the dive both successful and enjoyable. We will discuss specialized equipment, mental attitude, methods of research available to all divers, penetration, and much more. You will learn that the sport of wreck diving is performed on many different experience levels and that each dive is a learning experience.

Types of Wrecks

Throughout the world, there are wrecks of all types, sizes and ages. They range from ancient Egyptian vessels and old Spanish galleons, which are now often only piles of ballast stone, to warships, luxury liners, oil tankers, airplanes, barges, and even small cabin cruisers. Each is distinctly different and interesting for many reasons. For example, a wreck may appear to be nothing more than a big hulk of wood on the bottom, but through research and closer examination you can find that the wreck has significant historical value. Sport divers most often dive on fishing vessels, tug boats, or ships sunk during one of the World Wars.

Each wreck differs drastically, so as a wreck diver you must learn to judge the level of difficulty presented by each wreck so you can begin to understand the level of skill and equipment that each wreck requires.

As varied as the types of shipwrecks are, so are the water conditions surrounding them. A tug sunk in 15 feet (4.5 metres) of water might be a great beginner dive, but the same tug sunk in 60 feet (18 metres) should be left for the more experienced diver. As divers explore different types of wrecks, they soon notice that the deeper wrecks are often more intact than the wrecks closer to shore. These wrecks suffer greatly from the constant pounding from the sea, become broken up and are usually scattered over large areas.

Location

If the same tug boat was sunk in Grand Cayman and New York, the dives would be drastically different due to water clarity, temperature and currents or surge.

KNOWLEDGE SKILLS EQUIPMENT EXPERIENCE DIVER DIAMOND SSI SCUBA SCHOOLS INTERNATIONAL

Freshwater Wrecks of the Great Lakes

Before we go any farther we should point out that although most of our references are to wrecks in our oceans, there are many valuable freshwater wrecks. One of the best regions for freshwater wrecks, some up to 200 years old, is the Great Lakes Region of the United States and Canada. The wreckage you can find includes small wooden sailing ships and modern steel ocean-going freighters. One advantage to fresh water is that the wrecks

are generally in better condition than their salt water cousins, due to lack of corrosion from salt, colder water, and less wave action. While these wrecks are governed by state laws which prohibit or regulate the collection of artifacts, many divers consider the wrecks of the Great Lakes to be some of the finest in the world.

So although most wrecks do lie on our ocean floors, remember that many of the references we make to wrecks and wreck diving skills also apply to the many freshwater wrecks of the Great Lakes and other regions throughout the world.

1

3 Categories of Wrecks

Let's now take a look at the three categories that wrecks can be classified into and what each has to offer. We will discuss the categories of wrecks as artificial reefs, contemporary wrecks and historic wrecks.

- **Artificial Reefs.** The ocean's sandy sea floor often looks like a barren desert wasteland. Artificial reefs provide structure for sessile (stationary) invertebrates, such as mussels, barnacles, anemones, sponges and coral to adhere to. This carpet of growth supports mobile invertebrates including crabs, shrimp, snails, amphiods, starfish and sea urchins, which in turn are the primary source of food for larger fish.

  Artificial reefs can be made from any hard structure, such as old ships, concrete, car tires or even commercially fabricated units designed to attract fish. These reefs provide structure on otherwise barren sea beds. Marine life such as barnacles, anemones and soft coral quickly adhere to these structure. Crabs and lobsters make their home within the artificial habitat.

After only a few months most artificial reefs, especially the larger high profile ones, support entire ecosystems ranging from small bait fish to schooling pelagic predators.

Create a Reef

Many islands and waterfront areas have ongoing reef projects, continually sinking new vessels. These ships are usually derelicts, ex-military vessels or confiscated drug trafficking ships. Or, they may not be ships at all. Some artificial reefs are aircraft.

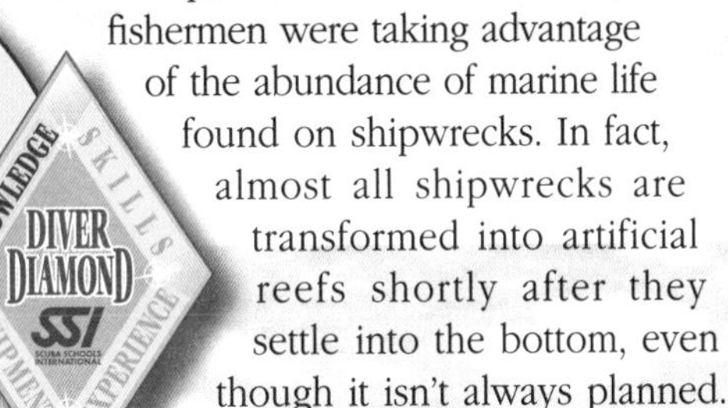

Long before the first planned artificial reef was placed on the ocean floor, fishermen were taking advantage of the abundance of marine life found on shipwrecks. In fact, almost all shipwrecks are transformed into artificial reefs shortly after they settle into the bottom, even though it isn't always planned. For classification reasons we will consider only wrecks actually sunk to form a reef in this section. As artificial reefs, shipwrecks offer divers even greater adventure and opportunity. These vessels are put through an elaborate preparation and cleaning process before being sunk. This assures that the sinking will only help, and not hurt, the undersea environment. Loose hatches, doors and other possible obstructions are usually removed to make the artificial reefs safer for divers. Whether for photography or just fish watching, artificial reefs created from ships provide divers with an ever growing assortment of fascinating shipwrecks to explore.

♦ **Contemporary.** Many of the wrecks found in coastal waters are considered contemporary wrecks. These are vessels like tugboats, fishing trawlers, and freighters that offer little historical significance but can provide first rate diving conditions. Many of these wrecks are still intact, providing an almost storybook shipwreck profile. These wrecks are often popular dive sites that are also enjoyed by local fishermen. As you explore different types of shipwrecks you will learn that each is unique. High profile wrecks seem to support a greater array of schooling baitfish while broken down, low-lying wooden wrecks harbor more lobsters and bottom fish. Each wreck also has its own unique features and opportunities for exploration and photography.

♦ **Historic.** While all wrecks over 50 years old are considered historic, age alone will not signify historic value. The vessel's identity, history and even construction type all play a role.

Good diving etiquette deems that divers should obey all laws and not disturb historic wrecks.

These wrecks are considered time capsules into our past and may hold clues and artifacts that will enhance our historical knowledge. These wrecks are important cultural resources that should be preserved for study and archaeological survey. However, all wrecks should be protected, not just historic sites. Wrecks are delicate, just like coral reefs, however, wrecks cannot grow back once they are damaged.

Shipwreck Laws and Protection

All shipwrecks in United States waters are covered by individual state laws under the proviso of the Abandoned Shipwreck Act. Some historic wrecks are even listed on the National Register of Historic Places. Other historic shipwrecks are protected as NOAA (National Oceanic and Atmospheric Administration) marine sanctuaries, and others are archaeological preserves.

You will need to obtain a permit before diving on some of these wrecks, while some wrecks only need a permit if you are planning on making an archaeological survey, or if you are planning on collecting any artifacts. Artifact collection is tightly controlled in the United States. Each state has its own laws in regards to artifact collection. Some states will allow you to collect artifacts if you turn them over to the state for research, and some states allow you to keep a percentage of the artifact's value. Other states allow you to keep a percentage of the artifacts, while turning over a percentage to the state. No state allows collection of artifacts for strictly personal use or collection.

Foreign sovereignties have their own laws regarding diving on shipwrecks and the collection of artifacts. International waters are covered by the International Court. These laws do not refer to debris or litter which is not associated with an historic or prehistoric site. Remember, these laws only exist to protect the resources that belong to the people of that country.

Researching the Wreck

Shipwreck research, or the ability to find out pertinent, accurate information on a shipwreck of interest, is an important part of wreck diving. It's nice to tell someone that you dove a paddle wheel steamship, but it's downright impressive to show them a historical photo and casually mention the exact date and cause of her sinking. Wreck research can also tie into identifying unknown shipwrecks.

There are many sources of information available to recreational sport divers, depending on the type of wreck and the date of her sinking. These sources range from the knowledge of local fisherman to articles, books and primary source material.

Obtaining the ship's name and approximate date of her sinking are the starting points of most research projects.

The ship's name may have been found by divers on her bell, or capstan cover, or the wreck may be known by a certain name, but her history may never have been traced.

Where to Collect Research

There are many places where the wreck diver can collect research data. Some of the places discussed here include dive stores, library archives, museums and clubs and societies. Depending on where you live there may be other research facilities available.

♦ **Dive Stores.** Local dive stores are probably the best and most accessible source of basic shipwreck information. Most stores sell books detailing the history and present condition of local shipwrecks, and many scuba magazines write articles each issue on famous shipwrecks. Also, the employees and instructors of the store are often knowledgeable as to the history of the wrecks and their present condition. Remember that as divers we are looking not only for historical facts pertaining to the vessel's sinking and history, but also to her present-day condition and any other pertinent diver information.

It's important to find out the depth and average visibility, whether the wreck is intact or scattered and if there is any surge or current on the site.

Professional dive store personnel will be able to provide all of this information as well as insight into the best areas on the wreck to explore.

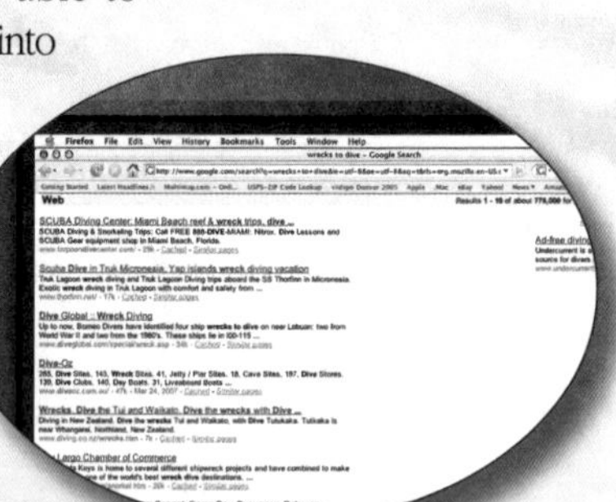

♦ **The Internet.** The Internet puts the world, and in this case, the underwater world, at your fingertips. Many public records as well as historical newspaper articles and photographs are available to everyone. You don't have to be a seasoned Internet Sleuth to find the information you're looking for, but it's a good idea to be organized and have a few notes ready to go before you begin your search.

Here are a few tips to help get you started:

1. **Organization is Key.** Keep your searches and information organized. There are few things more aggravating than having to redo research you've already done. For this reason, it's a good idea to know how you're going to organize your research before you begin. Create a folder on your computer dedicated to your search, keep everything related to the search in that folder and use clear file names.
2. **Internet Searching is an Art Form.** Many search engines query Internet websites based on keywords

the site designer placed into the website header. Because of this, it's best to use words and brief phrases for your searches. Too many words, or a long phrase may produce a small list of results; however, searching using very general terms may result in an inordinately large list of results. Don't get discouraged. Try searching everything at first. As you do more searches, you will quickly learn what works and what doesn't.

3. **General to Specific.** Start with general searches and narrow them down to specific keywords or phrases. Avoid starting a web search using very specific keywords or phrases unless you know that you will get the exact results, or "hits" that you're looking for. Also, if you limit your search to only a few specific keywords or phrases, you may be missing the big picture.

4. **Start with What You Know.** Write down all of the known keywords related to your search. For example, if looking for information on the "Titanic", you would want to include keywords like: The Vessel Name — "RMS Titanic;" the Shipbuilder — "Harland and Wolff;" the Ship Designer — "Thomas Andrews;" the Vessel Operator — "White Star Lines;" any known sister ships — "The Olympic;" vessels known to have assisted or communicated with the vessel — "Amerika," and "Carpathia" and so on.

5. **Keep a Research Log.** Write down all of the websites that you've visited, which ones had information useful to your search, and which ones did not. Also, it's likely that you'll find great sites with information on multiple wrecks and/or diving them. Bookmark these sites for an easy return in the future. Take screen shots and print out website pages if you need to. Remember, do everything and anything you can to stay organized.

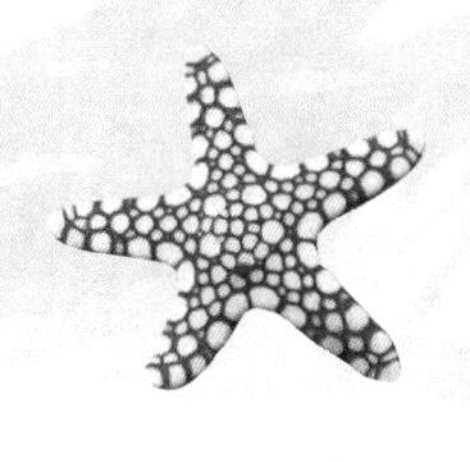

6. **Verify Your Research.** Anyone with a computer and Internet connection can create a website and post anything they want, fact or fabricated. Most reputable websites have valid information, but it's always a good idea to find other resources that can substantiate the information you find.

1

7. Have Fun! Like anything, researching wrecks will become what you make of it. Keep the fun of it at the forefront, and you'll be on your way to an exciting new, dry facet of your diving experience.

♦ **Library Archives.** Pay a visit to a nearby city or university library that carries back-issues of national and local newspapers on microfilm or microfiche. Major newspapers, such as *The New York Times,* can be valuable sources of information for the late 1800s and early 1900s. Almost all major shipwrecks are listed on the newspaper's front page or under titles such as marine casualties, explosions, disasters or shipping. Once at the library, the search can go in either of two directions. If you know the actual date of sinking, simply ask for the correct microfilm reel and search by page on that date. If the exact date of sinking is unknown, refer to the index volumes.

These volumes contain a wealth of information. Wrecks can actually be found under a variety of subtitles such as explosions, marine disasters, shipping, etc. Each year they may be listed under a different title, so you must scan all possible subtitles in each volume to find where they have listed shipwrecks in that volume. Once the wreck in question is found, the index gives you the date, page number and column number. This can then be easily found on microfilm. Photocopies can be made of all pertinent pages. Be sure to scan the following day's paper for continuous coverage.

The next source is any articles that have been written in either diving or fishing related magazines. These seem even more valuable when you consider that someone else has already gone through the trouble of doing the research. Don't forget to look in any books that may have been written on the particular subject you are studying. There are many well researched books with invaluable information available at local libraries or through dive shops.

Photo courtesy of the Los Angeles Maritime Museum Photo Archives

♦ **Museums.** Maritime Museums are one of the best possible sources for shipwreck research. Usually a letter requesting information is all that's needed. Remember that most museums are operating on limited budgets so don't request too much at one time. It's also very important to supply whatever information you have to begin the search.

The minimum information needed is the vessel's name and, if available, the date and location of her sinking.

If the wreck is a Naval vessel, also write to the Naval Armed Forces in your country. If it's a U.S. Coast Guard vessel, write to the United States Coast Guard. If the wreck is a foreign ship, try writing to a maritime museum in that country.

♦ **Disaster Records.** In the United States, most ships that have sunk have been recorded by the U.S. Coast Guard in a "loss record." Insurance companies have also kept fairly complete records of the sinkings to track their losses. Most of these records are considered Public Domain so they can be accessed through any of the U.S. National Archive locations and the Internet. These records can be complete and very helpful, or they may simply list that the ship has sunk, detailing no other information.

♦ **Clubs and Societies.** Clubs and historical societies offer wreck divers the opportunity to acquire a wealth of information that would otherwise require a substantial amount of time and research. It is highly recommended to take full advantage of the knowledge that is easily obtained here. Many clubs and historical societies are eager to assist divers in their efforts to find historical information, and are excited to learn from divers what condition the wreck is presently in. It becomes a win-win situation for both parties, each learning from the other's expertise. Also, many clubs post information about wrecks on their websites, and often have links to other websites with valuable information about vessel history.

Before you begin any research you should collect the basic information on the wreck as a starting place. If you are planning on working with a museum, the government, or an archaeologist, the worksheet listed in the appendix will allow you to collect the type of information they need for the search. This sheet will allow you both to speak the same language, allowing for more efficient communication. This worksheet is the standard form used by the Advisory Council on Underwater Archaeology.

1

Shipwreck Information Sources

Below and on the next pages is a listing of some sources of shipwreck information. This is only a partial listing and it may not be completely up to date. If you know of other sources in your area, or if any of the information below changes, please write to SSI at 2619 Canton Court, Fort Collins, Colorado USA 80525-4498.

By the time you're done, you will have a folder full of photo copies from different sources. No doubt you will also

Australia

Mitchell Library
Macquarie Street
Sydney, NSW, Australia

Maritime Services Board of Australia
207 Kent Street
Sydney, NSW, Australia

Maritime Museum
Darling Harbour
Sydney, NSW, Australia

Bermuda

Bermuda Maritime Museum
Po Box MA 273
Mangrove Bay, Bermuda
MA BX

Canada

Canadian Hydrographic Service Surveys and Mapping Branch
No 8 Temporary Building
Ottawa, Ontario Canada

Wheelhouse Maritime Museum
222 Cumberland Street
Ottawa 2,
Ontario, Canada K1N 7H5

Marine Museum of the Great Lakes at Kingston
55 Ontario St.
Kingston, Ontario Canada
K7L 2Y2

Public Archives of Canada
Trade and Communications
Records Center
395 Wellington Street
Ottawa, Ontario Canada K1A ON3

England

Imperial War Museum
Lambeth Rd
London, England, SE1 6HZ

National Maritime Museum
Greenwich
London, England SE1 9NF

Cunard Museum
University of Liverpool
Po Box 147
Liverpool, England L69 3BX

Spain

Archives Of The Indies
Seville, Spain

Museo Naval
Madrid, Spain

Museo National
Darling Harbour
Madrid, Spain

United States (General)

Library of Congress
Geography and Map Division
Washington, DC 20540

Mariners Museum Library
Newport News, VA 23606

Maritime Administration
Division of Reserve Fleet
Fleet Disposal Branch
Department of Commerce
Building
Washington, DC 20230

National Archives and Records
Attention: NCRD
8th and Pennsylvania Ave,
MW
General Administration
Washington, DC 20408

National Maritime Museum
Porter Shaw Library
Foot of Polk Street
San Francisco, CA 94109

National Ocean Service
Hydrographic Surveys Branch
6001 Executive Boulevard
Rockville, MD 20852

Naval Historical Center (SH)
Building 220-2
Washington Navy Yard
Washington, DC 20374

Peabody Museum of Salem
Phillips Library
East India Square
Salem, MA 01970

Philadelphia Maritime
Museum Library
321 Chestnut Street
Philadelphia, PA 19106

Smithsonian Institution
Museum of American History
Washington, DC 20560

Steamship Historical Society
of America
University of Baltimore
Library
1420 Maryland Ave
Baltimore, MD 21201

South Street Seaport Museum
207 Front Street
New York, NY 10038

Texas Antiquities Committee
Box 12276
Capitol Station
Austin, TX 78711

Great Lakes Region

Burton Historical Collection
Detroit Public Library
5201 Woodward Ave
Detroit, MI 48202

Dossin Great Lakes Museum
Great Lakes Maritime
Institute
Belle Isle
Detroit, MI 48207

Great Lakes Charts
630 Federal Building
U.S. Courthouse
Detroit MI 48226

Great Lakes Historical Society
480 Main Street
Vermilion, OH 44089

Institute for Great Lakes
Research
Bowling Green State
University
12764 Levis Parkway
Perrysburg, OH 43551

Runge Collection
Milwaukee Public Library
814 Wisconsin Ave.
Milwaukee, WI 53233

have conflicting information as to the time, date and number of casualties. Usually, the cause of these discrepancies among materials is typing errors from the original articles printed about the wreck. Articles with bad information then become a source of information for the next author who is writing on the same subject, creating a vicious cycle of false information. As a researcher, accept the responsibility to be as accurate as possible. Usually going back to your earliest source for verifying information assures accuracy. If available, check out any conflicting information by going back to the original Coast Guard or Life Saving Service reports. These are available at some maritime museums.

Once finished, share your knowledge and research with the sport divers in your area. It will make wreck diving more rewarding and enjoyable for all. Researching wrecks is a great way to spend your time when you are not able to go diving. It increases your knowledge, and helps satisfy your diving appetite.

Summary

Unlike other diving activities, wreck diving offers a glimpse into the past. All wrecks, whether artificial reefs, contemporary wrecks or historical wrecks, have their own story to tell and each offers unique opportunities for exploration and photography.

However, remember that all wrecks in the United States are covered by individual state laws and worldwide by international maritime laws as well as those enacted by foreign sovereignties. In the US, many wrecks are listed on the National Register of Historic Places and others are protected as marine sanctuaries and archeological preserves. Be sure to investigate and abide by the laws that govern the wreck(s) you plan to dive.

When researching a wreck, take advantage of the multitude of resources available including the Internet, libraries, museums, disaster records, dive clubs, historical wreck societies, and of course your local dive center. Keep your research as organized as possible, and have fun! In Section Two we'll discuss various wreck diving equipment and its use.

Section I Review Questions

1. This course is designed to help the wreck diver gain an understanding of how to judge wreck sites in order to decide the ______________________________ that is required to make the dive both safe and enjoyable.

2. As divers explore different types of wrecks, they soon notice that the deeper wrecks are often more intact than the wrecks ______________________________ .

3. Loose hatches, doors and other possible obstructions are usually removed to make the ________________ safer for divers.

4. While all wrecks over 50 years old are considered historic, age alone will not signify historic value. The vessel's ____________ , ____________ and even ________________ all play a role.

5. All shipwrecks in United States waters are covered by individual state laws under the proviso of the ________________ ______________________ .

6. Remember that as divers we are looking not only for historical facts pertaining to the vessel's sinking and history, but also to her ______________________ .

7. In the United States, most ships that have sunk have been recorded by the ______________________________ ________________ .

8. Many clubs and historical societies are eager to assist divers in their efforts to find ______________________________ ________________

SSI SCUBA SCHOOLS INTERNATIONAL

Wreck Diving Equipment

Section 2 Objectives

After completing this section you will be able to describe:

- Basic wreck diving equipment,
- The recommended method for equipment placement when wreck diving,
- How to secure your equipment for wreck diving,
- What safety lines are, when to use safety lines and how to use them.

The equipment used for wreck diving will vary from location to location. On shallow scattered wrecks, a single cylinder of air may be sufficient, but on intact or deeper offshore shipwrecks, double cylinders or the addition of a pony bottle may be necessary. Likewise, diving in the warm clear waters of the Caribbean may only require a bathing suit, but cold water divers often choose to wear dry suits all year round. Take these regional differences into consideration as we discuss the equipment needed for wreck diving. The selection of wreck diving equipment is also a highly individual matter. Just remember, we want to streamline ourselves as much as possible to reduce drag, to permit easier swimming with less fatigue, and to eliminate the possibility of becoming snagged on the wreck.

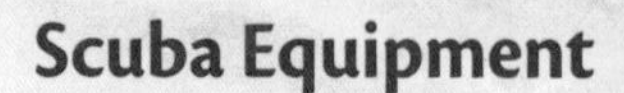

Scuba Equipment

When diving on wrecks that are in relatively mild water conditions and at reasonable depths you will only need basic scuba equipment.

More complicated wreck dives often require more sophisticated equipment.

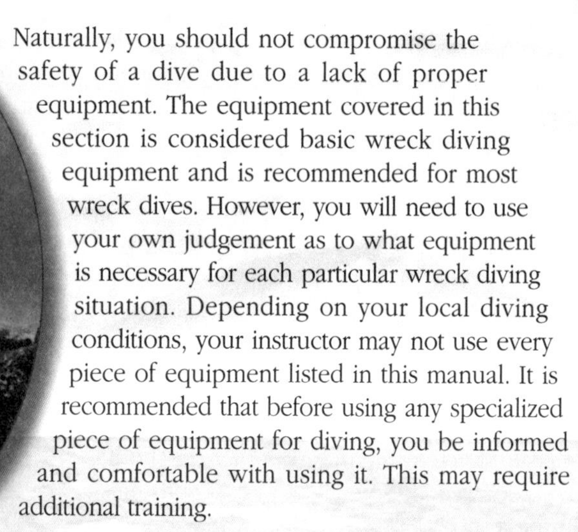

Naturally, you should not compromise the safety of a dive due to a lack of proper equipment. The equipment covered in this section is considered basic wreck diving equipment and is recommended for most wreck dives. However, you will need to use your own judgement as to what equipment is necessary for each particular wreck diving situation. Depending on your local diving conditions, your instructor may not use every piece of equipment listed in this manual. It is recommended that before using any specialized piece of equipment for diving, you be informed and comfortable with using it. This may require additional training.

A wreck diver's equipment consists of the necessary thermal protection for the environment, back-up equipment needed for the depth, and additional equipment to help make the wreck dive safer.

All of this equipment must be located so it is easily accessible and not dangling, possibly causing the diver to get snagged on the wreckage.

Dangling equipment is also more likely to get damaged, and to damage any delicate wreckage. Let's start now by examining some basic dive equipment and some modifications that are used in this exciting sport of wreck diving.

Dry Suit Diving

Your SSI Dive Center offers the SSI Dry Suit Diving specialty program in which you will learn proper dry suit diving techniques, dry suit maintenance, and the benefits of diving dry.

KNOWLEDGE SKILLS EQUIPMENT EXPERIENCE DIVER DIAMOND SSI SCUBA SCHOOLS INTERNATIONAL

ce

Exposure Suits

No matter what type of wreck you are diving, it is recommended that an exposure suit is worn for both warmth and protection. As you learned in your *Open Water Diver* class, water conducts heat away from our bodies 25 times faster than air. This means that even warm water can start to feel cold after a few minutes under water.

There are a variety of exposure suits on the market, the one you use will depend on the temperature and depth of the water you're diving in. Exposure suits vary drastically in design, thickness and thermal protection based on the type of diving they are designed for. In warm waters, divers may choose to wear a lycra suit or a 2 to 3 mm short wet suit. Cold water divers will prefer 5 to 6 mm wet suits with hoods, boots, and gloves, or dry suits. Dry suits also come in many designs and materials. Purchase the warmest, best fitting suit that fits your budget. It is important to be warm and comfortable so you can enjoy your dive.

Many shipwrecks look like huge junk yards scattered across the ocean floor. You should consider wearing some type of exposure suit for protection from cuts and splinters, even if the water is warm. A farmer-john pant is one alternative in warm water to protect the legs from contact with wreckage.

Wrecks are also hard on exposure suits, especially the knee area. Knee pads will greatly extend the life of a dry, or wet suit. Pull-up style knee pads offer the added benefit of inhibiting some air from entering the feet of dry suits. This reduced buoyancy in the foot area allows for easier swimming and a more comfortable dive.

Remember that wrecks, especially historic wrecks, can be delicate. A protective suit and gloves do not give the diver a license to "manhandle" the wreck. Treat these delicate wrecks as you would coral.

♦ **Glove Care.** To increase the life of neoprene gloves or mitts, use a thin coat of an adhesive such as Aqua Seal® on the finger tip area of each glove. Be careful not to apply too much glue, or you will lose dexterity due to the stiff hardening substance. To protect your hands when wreck diving, gloves of some kind are a must. In colder waters where gloves or mitts are worn, the abrasiveness of wreck diving is quickly noticed by the wear-and-tear on the finger tips. After only a few dives, chunks of neoprene seem to vanish, leaving only cold bare flesh to face the elements.

To properly apply, squeeze a small portion onto a paper plate, then spread the glue onto each desired area with a plastic knife. Without any delay, scrape off as much of the glue as possible leaving only a thin abrasive resistant coating. This coating will easily double, if not triple, the life of your neoprene gloves.

The Air Delivery System

Wreck divers need to take a few safety precautions into consideration when choosing an air delivery system. Because many wrecks lie in deeper water, the same considerations when choosing an Air Delivery System for deep diving adhere — a dependable system that breathes well at depth. Back-up systems become even more important to wreck divers though. Wreck divers not only have to deal with increased depth, but also the increased possibility of entanglement and entrapment. Wreck divers should keep their cylinders, air delivery system and back-up systems maintained and in proper working condition.

♦ **Back-Up Systems.** Redundancy of the air delivery system is one way to help make wreck dives safer. How much redundancy is required is based on the type of wreck you will be exploring. Shallow, warm water wrecks may not require anything more than the standard alternate air source.

Many wreck divers also like to carry separate independent air sources such as a pony bottle. Smaller systems such as the Spare Air® do not provide enough emergency air for most wreck dives and are not recommended. Some very experienced wreck divers who dive deep wrecks in limited visibility, or who penetrate into wrecks, will carry double cylinders, such as two Aluminium 80s, each with its own second-stage regulator and

2

SSI TechXR

SSI TechXR (Technical eXtended Range) programs are designed for the adventurous diver who wants to learn how to utilize new equipment and gain the greater Skills, Knowledge and Experience required for extended range and deep wreck diving. Check out www.diveSSI.com, or talk to your SSI Dive Center for more information about SSI TechXR training.

KNOWLEDGE SKILLS DIVER DIAMOND EQUIPMENT EXPERIENCE SSI SCUBA SCHOOLS INTERNATIONAL alternate air source. The idea is to have extra air should an emergency occur. If a diver becomes entangled there is additional air until help arrives. If a diver accidentally goes into decompression, additional air is available for safety stops. If a diver becomes lost, there is extra air available until the anchor line can be found.

- **Alternate Air Source Placement and Identification:** The additional safety an alternate air source offers is often reduced because divers don't take the time to mount the second-stage in a convenient, easily reached and secure location. Having the mouthpiece float behind you or drag in the mud is only a little better than not having one at all. Not only can your equipment become clogged, but it's also not easily accessible when needed. Your alternate air sources should be located around your chest area. In fact, if you were to draw an imaginary triangle from your waist up to your shoulders, your extra second stages should be mounted within it. Divers should also be able to distinguish between second-stages. This is extremely important, especially when using double cylinders or a pony bottle. If the second-stages were not marked, a diver could easily be using the pony bottle instead of the main cylinder.

There are many methods of identification. One way is to use a different style, brand or color for the alternate air source, or to use color coded hose protectors. This can be carried one step further by color coding the corresponding pressure gauge with the same color as the second-stage regulator.

Each second-stage regulator should also have a quick disconnect release. We do not recommended that you store your alternate air source in a buoyancy compensator pocket because it takes too long to get it out when it's needed. There are a number of quick release devices on the market which are available from your local SSI Dive Center. Some non-commercial methods of securing the second-stage include hooking an alligator clip from your BC to the mouthpiece, or hooking the second-stage to a loop of surgical tubing worn loosely around your neck. There is no searching around for your alternate air source with this method because it's always directly under your chin. Any method works as long as it makes the second-stage regulator easy to find and disconnect in an emergency.

Instruments

It is recommended that the wreck diver carry a high-quality, appropriately-maintained dive computer. Alternately, the wreck diver may carry analogue instruments including a submersible pressure gauge (SPG), depth gauge, and timer.

If you are diving with a computer that combines your depth gauge, pressure gauge and bottom timer, you may want to carry a back up of each of these instruments in case your computer fails during the dive. Any time a computer fails on a dive, it is recommended that you end the dive and immediately ascend to the surface.

The AAUS (the American Academy of Underwater Sciences) and many computer manufacturers recommend that you complete a 24-hour surface interval after computer failure to completely off-gas any nitrogen from your system.

Weight Systems

We have always been taught that weights are expendable, and should be dropped quickly in an emergency situation. This still applies to wreck divers—but only when they are not in an overhead environment. If a wreck diver's weight system release mechanism got snagged and released by a piece of wreckage, a serious problem could result.

If you are using an integrated weight system, be sure that the release mechanism, or handle is securely fastened, and that it cannot get snagged on any wreckage. Many integrated weight systems have a built in redundant locking mechanism that help ensure that the mechanism is released only when you want it to be. Talk with your SSI Dive Center or instructor for more information about integrated weight systems, or if you have questions about how your system functions.

If you use a weight belt instead of an integrated weight system, one option is to install two buckles on your weight belt. Only engage the first buckle while exploring outside the wreck and for standard ascents and descents. Secure the second buckle before entering any overhead environment, or tight spaces. This will provide added security while allowing for an emergency outside of the wreck, and on the surface.

Special Equipment

While many of these pieces of special wreck diving equipment may seem standard to many divers, they all have special uses to the wreck diver. Because of this, it is recommended that you carry these pieces of equipment on every dive. As we have mentioned before, wreck diving can be a potentially dangerous activity, so it is important that wreck divers are properly equipped and trained in the use of their equipment.

Slate and Pencil

A small slate and pencil can come in handy for underwater communication, or for making notes about the wreck. You may want to note special features, draw a map, or you may simply want to write a note to your buddy. The slate can be stored in a pocket, mounted on your instrument console, or you can also purchase a slate that fits over your forearm.

The Diver's Tool

It is essential for all wreck divers to wear at least one diver's tool. Also, a back-up is highly recommended. Almost any brand will do, but bear in mind that the quality of the tool is usually directly related to the price.

- **Tool Features.** When shopping for a diver's tool, the type of alloy the blade is made from should be taken into consideration. Stainless steel varies greatly in its strength, durability and rust inhibiting factors. For example, 304 series stainless offers excellent resistance to rust but it needs to be sharpened often. Plus, it should not be used for prying. 440 series stainless contains less chrome and is less resistant to rust. This high carbon alloy is very tough and holds a sharp edge longer than the 304 series. The negatives are that the blade will rust and it is a little brittle. Tools made of 440 stainless should not be used for prying either.

As a primary tool, it is recommended that you wear a medium size blade, solidly constructed with a portion of the blade serrated. This serration allows for easier cutting of heavy rope. Other options available in diver's tools include ground-in line cutters and a solid metal butt on the back end of the handle to use as a tap hammer.

♦ **Tool Placement.** Your diver's tools can be attached to your instrument console, your leg, or your BC. As a side note, many wreck divers choose to attach their leg-mounted tools with surgical tubing. By doing so, they simply pull the tools up their leg to the predetermined location and do not have to fumble with small buckles when suiting up. Other divers mount neoprene pockets to their suits. Another method uses elastic straps and quick release buckle connections. Mount your primary and back-up tools in separate locations so you can access one or the other at all times.

♦ **Tool Maintenance.** Sharpening is the most important maintenance you can perform on your diver's tool. A wreck diver's tool must be very sharp at all times. This is because, in and around shipwrecks they encounter monofilament lines, discarded penetration lines, anchor lines, and nets and ropes of all sizes. Each of these could be potentially hazardous if entanglement occurs, and a good sharp diver's tool will ensure an easy escape. A back-up serves the same function in case your main diver's tool is lost or cannot be easily reached.

One way to sharpen your blade is simply to buy a good cross hatched fine metal file. Don't try to get a perfect edge; simply file both sides of the blade and leave the ragged razor-like burr on the edge. It's this burr that will allow you to slice through rope better than a honed blade. The one negative with this manner of sharpening is that the blade will dull rapidly, so it will be necessary to sharpen it often. It is recommended that you sharpen your blades before each day of diving. Other more sophisticated sharpening methods include honing or stone sharpening.

Lights

As a wreck diver, you will need two different types of lights and, of course, back-up lights. Your primary light should be a powerful, dependable, wide-beam light which is capable of illuminating a large area of the wreck. This primary light should have a burn time longer than the planned duration of the dive. H.I.D. lights are a good choice for your primary light source. A back-up, wide-beam light is also strongly advised. Your secondary light should be a smaller spot light that can be used to look deep into holes.

Remember that the location of these lights is critical. Each should be located in a secure place that doesn't cause a possible snag, yet allows easy access.

If you enjoy lobstering around shipwrecks, try taping a lobster size gauge to a small narrow-beam spot light. This combines two items of equipment and makes it quick and easy to find, catch and measure lobsters without fumbling around for a gauge. Remember, as with night diving, it is important never to shine your light into your own or anyone else's eyes. This would have an immediate negative effect on your buddy's vision.

Head and Helmet Lights

Wreck divers, as well as night divers and cave divers, have found that having a light or lights mounted on their head allows them to keep their hands free, while still being able to see. There are many types of helmet lights available through your local dive store, or divers can use a little ingenuity to modify a light so it can be head-mounted.

This setup allows you to have a back-up light in a location which is out of the way — on your head. These lights come in very handy when working, or when your hands are needed to hold a tether line reel.

One drawback to head-mounted lights is that they tend to increase the amount of head movement. When diving in a dry suit, this can increase the amount of leakage through the neck seal of the suit. This problem is usually only temporary until the diver becomes familiar enough with the equipment to find movements that don't cause leakage. Another drawback is that head-mounted lights make it easy to shine the light in your buddy's eyes.

More Info

For more information about primary and secondary lights, we recommend enrolling in an SSI Night and Limited Visibility specialty program. Contact your SSI Dive Center for details.

When choosing a light to be head-mounted, make sure it is easy to switch on. Then decide, based on the type of diving you do, whether you prefer a large main light or a smaller back-up light. Cave diving lights are also excellent for head mounting. These units have remote battery packs which are mounted to a harness or your cylinder so they are extremely powerful and long lasting.

Goodie Bag

Goodie bags, which are also referred to as bug bags, game bags, tool bags, or catch bags, are simply mesh bags that divers use to carry tools and other items. Wreck divers should keep their bag wrapped up and in the closed position when starting their dive. The reason is that an open bag tends to snag on each and every piece of wreckage you swim over. When you need to use the bag, you can snap it onto the lower portion of your buoyancy compensator or harness, so it floats above your legs. This keeps the bag from dragging on the wreck.

Some divers prefer to use a 1/2" (12.5 mm) rope instead of a harness. The D-Ring rope is approximately two feet long and is spliced into a loop on one end and has a D-Ring spliced on the other end. The rope is attached to the diver's cylinder valve by placing the loop over the valve before the second-stage regulator is attached. This line, which usually hangs over the left shoulder, is used to clip the goodie bag.

One other note on bags: If you are interested in lobsters, buy a bag that has nylon material on the top and mesh on the bottom. This allows you to insert the lobster easily into the bag, without all of his legs getting caught in the mesh.

The SSI Equipment Service Program

The Equipment Service Program, which is available through your SSI Dive Center, is a complete maintenance program designed to keep the components of your Total Diving System performing to the best of their potential. Below is an explanation of each of the services that make up the SSI Equipment Service Program.

Air Delivery System Protection

Regulators are totally disassembled and cleaned in a special cleaning solution. High-pressure and low-pressure seats are replaced along with all dynamic o-rings, exhaust valves, and high pressure filters. Performance tests are conducted to manufacturer warranty specifications.

Nitrox Air Delivery System Protection

This is the same as Air Delivery System Protection, but is performed on Nitrox equipment. A green Nitrox hose sleeve is used to mark your Nitrox Air Delivery System rather than a yellow hose sleeve.

Information System Protection

Submersible pressure gauges, depth gauges, pressure activated dive timers, and dive computers are checked for accuracy in a pressure vessel, and the indicated readings versus true readings are noted.

Buoyancy Control System Protection

Buoyancy compensators are inspected for leaks, buckle strap tension and bladder seam integrity. Inflator mechanisms are disassembled, cleaned and rebuilt, the inner bladder rinsed with BC conditioner and over-pressure release valves are cleaned and tested for proper operation, all to manufacturer warranty specifications.

Visual Inspection Protection (and Visual Plus®)

Annually, cylinders are inspected internally and externally for rust, corrosion and cracks to the standards of DOT and CGA. It is suggested that aluminium cylinders be tested with

Visual Plus to ensure the integrity and strength of the neck and threads.

Exposure System Protection

Services are available for exposure suits (wet and dry). Minor repairs are done in house and alterations are done with the original manufacturer.

When you have your equipment serviced or repaired, take along your SSI Total DiveLog so the technician can record the service.

Securing Your Equipment

Wrecks are fragile, whether they look like it or not, and dangling equipment can easily damage a wreck, whether it is metal or wood.

Wreck divers should make sure that all their air delivery system hoses are streamlined to reduce the chance of hoses snagging, or mouthpieces and instruments hitting the wreckage.

Route all hoses as close to your body as possible, and attach all mouthpieces and instruments to your BC. Depending on your equipment, this can be easy or may require the use of plastic wire ties, Velcro straps, snaps or special equipment holders. The same precautions should be used when carrying excess equipment such as lights and bags. Streamline these as much as possible.

Equipment

The next time you're on a charter boat, take a look around at how each diver's equipment is set up. If you see anything interesting, ask how it works or why it's rigged in that manner. You will be surprised at how many tricks and ideas you can pick up.

There are few rules regarding the location of items such as back-up lights and tether line reels, but all divers should carefully plan where each piece of equipment is to be placed. For example, a back-up light is useless unless it can be easily and quickly located, even in the worst conditions. Divers can be quite creative and ingenious in locating such items.

When streamlining equipment, make sure not to reduce your access to it in case of an emergency.

Snaps and Clips

One good method of attaching equipment is with brass snaps and D-Rings. Quick spring snaps are not the best choice. The problem is that these snaps can easily twist and cause the snap to release. For example, a diver who had a quick snap attached to his weight belt could easily get hooked onto the dive boat's anchor line while descending. Another disadvantage of the spring snap is that it is responsible for a significant amount of equipment loss. For example, if the snap is clipped onto a strap or even a small diameter D-Ring, the snap can be opened unintentionally by twisting it so that the spring gate is forced open. It is recommended that you use either stainless steel locking carabiners or brass snaps with a sliding gate.

If you choose to use brass snaps and/or clips, be sure to attach these items with line that you can cut with your diver's tool in the event of a snag or emergency.

Marking Your Equipment

It's also a good idea to mark each piece of your equipment with your name. This is very important on busy charter boats when everyone has equipment that is similar. This way, if something is lost, hopefully it will be found and returned.

Safety Lines

Safety lines for wreck diving should be flexible and water resistant. Nylon lines serve this purpose well. Hemp or cotton rope is unreliable (they will eventually rot in water) and become heavy and unmanageable when they are wet. This is unacceptable for safety lines, except in the case of the up-line, where biodegradability is what you want.

Most of the safety lines mentioned here pertain to boat diving, which is the most common transportation method used for wreck diving. Other lines are personal lines that are carried on the wreck diver when diving. While these lines are not required, they can all add to the safety of the wreck diving experience.

Tether Line Reel

A tether line reel is a valuable piece of equipment for the wreck diver. It can be used as a safety line or buddy line in limited visibility to keep the buddy team together. It can be used as a navigational tool when exploring the wreck, and it can act as an emergency up-line should the diver be unable to return to the anchor line. This reel can also be used for search and recovery or underwater mapping of the wreck site. The many uses make a tether line a valuable tool.

In the case of limited visibility, the line can serve as a guide to and from the dive boat's anchor. Simply hook the line onto the anchor line before you begin to explore. Some divers choose to tie knots in the line every 10 feet (3 metres). By counting the knots in the line as it is let out, you can tell how far you are from the anchor. When it is time to return to the anchor, simply reel in the line as you swim.

Since dive reels were originally designed for cave diving in fresh water, it's important to use a reel that was specifically designed to withstand the rigors and abrasive environment of salt water wreck diving. These wreck reels are available with anodized aluminium or stainless steel construction and contain all of the desired design features such as sufficient line capacity, lock down screw, and contoured winding knob.

Most tether line reels normally use a number 36 white braided nylon line. This line may be sufficient for cave diving but it is too thin for wreck diving. Wreck reels should contain a 1/8" (2.5 mm) diamond braided nylon.

Nylon is preferred because it is strong and somewhat abrasion resistant, because it is highly visible and because it sinks.

If a floating line were used, it would have the tendency to get tangled in the diver's feet as it was unreeled, and it would not stay where it was laid out.

The reel should be held with one finger firmly on the spool so that the spool turns only when there is tension on the line. The line should never be clipped off and allowed to play out unattended. When reeling in the line, reel just fast enough to maintain a constant tension on the line. Make sure the line feeds evenly across the spool face to prevent jamming. Remember, just having a reel is not a substitute for proper training in how to use it.

Up-Line Reel

Up-line reels are also commonly referred to as Jersey Reels, because they were first used in New Jersey. This reel is separate from the tether line reel, and is simply a basic reel that can be carried on your cylinder for use in emergencies. Unlike other lines, this line is made from hemp so it is inexpensive and biodegradable.

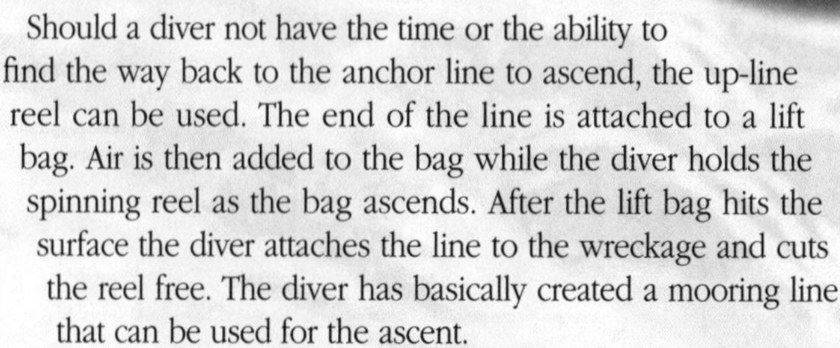

Should a diver not have the time or the ability to find the way back to the anchor line to ascend, the up-line reel can be used. The end of the line is attached to a lift bag. Air is then added to the bag while the diver holds the spinning reel as the bag ascends. After the lift bag hits the surface the diver attaches the line to the wreckage and cuts the reel free. The diver has basically created a mooring line that can be used for the ascent.

The other way to use the up-line for ascending is to tie the loose end of the line to the wreck and swim to the surface, unreeling the line as you ascend.

The diver is able to ascend on the up-line because of the upward tension created by having the line attached to the wreck below. If there is a strong current you will need to have more line in the reel than you are deep because you will ascend at an angle. For example, if you are 60 feet (18 metres) deep, your reel should have at least 100 feet (300 metres) of line. Because of the strong current, you ascend at an angle and may end up some distance behind the boat. The dive boat should be equipped with a surface current line or a trail line that you can swim to.

Upon surfacing, the line is cut from the reel and left attached to the wreck. Because the line is hemp, it will break apart and dissolve in the water. Because of this biodegradability, it is preferable to use the Jersey Reel as an up-line instead of your tether line reel.

2

Descent/Ascent Line

The anchor line is the line which tethers the boat to the anchor. Often, the anchor line is used as the ascent line which the divers can follow back to the boat. In some cases, such as when moorings are used, a separate line is dropped for an ascent line. This line can be a weighted drop line that is either attached to the boat, or a float on the surface that is weighted or attached to the wreck.

The use of descent lines is covered in more detail in Section 4, Diving the Wreck.

Current Line (Granny Line)

The dive boat may also choose to set up a current line, which is also referred to as a Granny Line. Current lines are used by divers to assist them in getting from the boat to the anchor line in current situations. The current line should be attached from the stern of the dive boat to the anchor with a shackle and weighted so it drops to about 20 feet (6 metres). The line must be within the divers grasp after entering the water. The divers can then pull themselves along the current line to reach the anchor line. This will save a lot of time and energy when diving in a current.

The current line works well, especially when divers are entering the water using a step-in, or giant stride, entry. This is because the diver has better control over where he is going to land. Sometimes divers using entries such as the back roll can get caught in a floating granny line and have to adopt other techniques.

Trail Line (Surface Current Line)

The trail line runs a distance off the stern of the dive boat with an inner tube or flotation device attached to the opposite end. Because the line trails behind the boat it always flows with the current. Thus divers have a safe rendezvous point prior to reboarding the dive boat that allows them to float, and not fight the current.

Cross-Wreck Line

In heavy current or poor visibility situations, a cross-wreck line can be tied from the bow to the stern of the wreck, increasing the diver's safety while traversing the wreck. In parks and on archaeological sites, the cross-wreck line is often called a tag line.

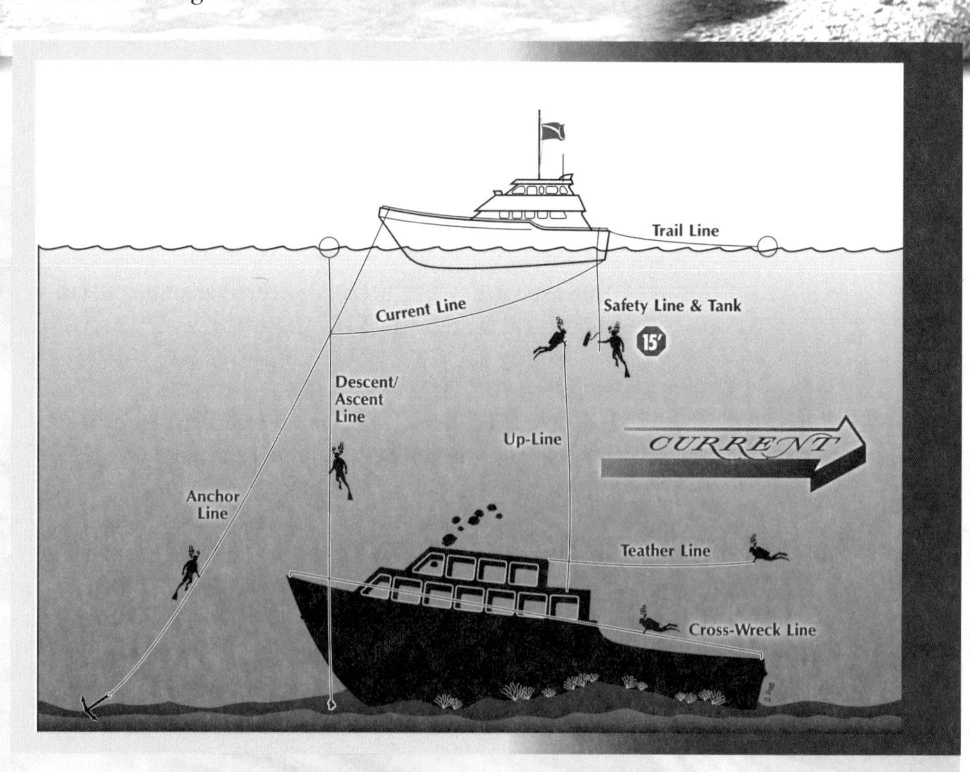

Safety Cylinder and Line

When deep diving on a deep wreck, you should have an extra cylinder with two second-stages tied off at 15 feet (5 metres) to a separate safety line, or to the ascent

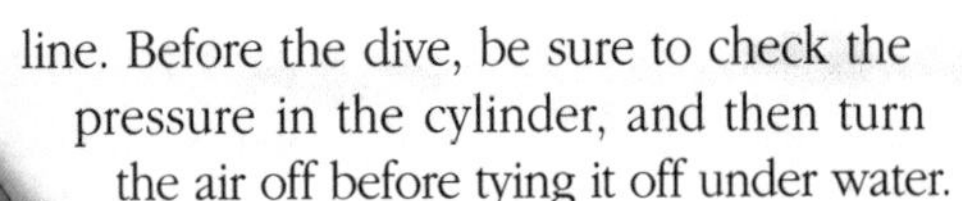

line. Before the dive, be sure to check the pressure in the cylinder, and then turn the air off before tying it off under water. Do not count on using this air as part of your dive plan; it is there strictly for emergency use should you run low on air during your safety stop.

The line should be weighted so it hangs straight down. In fact, you may want to put some extra weight belts on the line in case a diver is too positively buoyant at the end of the dive to maintain the safety stop.

Summary

Equipment for recreational wreck diving is generally the same equipment you would use for the equivalent type of conditions on any other dive. However, there are additional, specialized pieces of equipment specific to wreck diving.

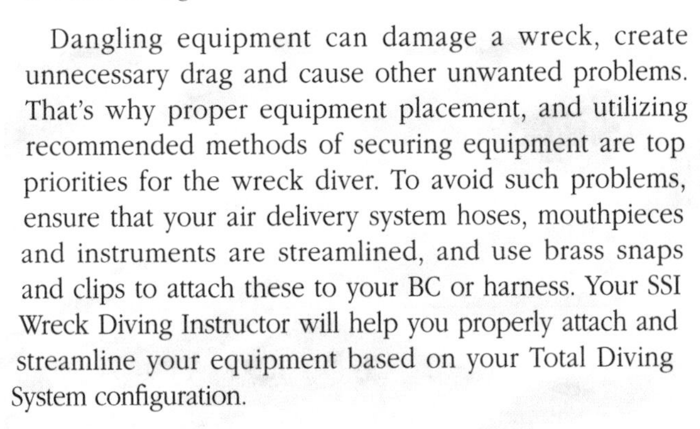

Dangling equipment can damage a wreck, create unnecessary drag and cause other unwanted problems. That's why proper equipment placement, and utilizing recommended methods of securing equipment are top priorities for the wreck diver. To avoid such problems, ensure that your air delivery system hoses, mouthpieces and instruments are streamlined, and use brass snaps and clips to attach these to your BC or harness. Your SSI Wreck Diving Instructor will help you properly attach and streamline your equipment based on your Total Diving System configuration.

In Section Three we will discuss methods for getting to wreck sites, and how to locate the wreck once you've arrived at the general location.

Section 2 Review Questions

1. You will need to use your own judgement as to what equipment is necessary for each particular ______________________________ ______________________________.

2. No matter what type of wreck you are diving, it is recommended that an exposure suit is worn for both ______________________________ ______________________________.

3. Redundancy of the air system is one way to help make wreck dives safer. How much redundancy is required is based on ______________________________ .

2

4. Mount your primary and back-up knives in separate locations so you can ______________________________ ______________________________.

5. Your primary light should be a powerful, dependable, wide-beam light which is capable of ______________________________ ______________________________. This primary light should have a burn time longer than the ______________________________ ______________________________.

6. Wrecks are fragile, whether they look like it or not, and dangling equipment can easily ______________________________ ______________________________.

7. In the case of limited visibility, the tether line reel can serve as a guide to and from the ______________________________ ______________________________.

8. Should a diver not have the time or the ability to find the way back to the anchor line to ascend, the ______________________________ ______________________________ can be used.

9. Current lines are used by divers to assist them in getting from the boat to ______________________________ ______________ in current situations.

10. When deep diving on a wreck, you should have an __________ ______________________________ ______________ tied off at 15 feet (4.5 metres) to a separate safety line, or to the ascent line.

Locating the Wreck

Section 3 Objectives

After completing this section you will be able to:

- Describe options for traveling to wreck sites,
- List various methods for locating shipwrecks.

Locating a shipwreck on the ocean floor is not a simple task. The easiest way to dive a shipwreck is to sign on to a charter dive boat. The captains who operate dive boats have extensive knowledge and experience. They locate shipwrecks with sophisticated electronics aboard their vessel. While charter dive boats may be the easiest, other less accessible wreck sites can be found either by swimming off the beach or using smaller personal boats. Of course you must have the correct equipment, seamanship and experience to locate a wreck site successfully.

Getting to the Wreck

There are various ways to get to the wreck, including traveling by boat or swimming from shore. As mentioned earlier, charter boats provide the easiest option because all the work of navigation and location is done for you.

Charter Boats

Dive boats vary drastically in size, style and design, depending on what type of conditions they were designed for. When dealing with commercial charter boats, divers should have to check only to see that the captain is licensed and that the vessel is certified for the number of customers on board. Divers can usually just relax and wait for the captain to anchor up to the wreck and then enjoy the dive. Charter operations often run so smoothly that to the beginner, finding and anchoring over a wreck site looks easy. Don't be fooled, locating a shipwreck miles off shore requires not only the proper electronic equipment, but also the knowledge, experience and expertise to use them. For the novice, or even the experienced wreck diver, signing on to a charter dive excursion is the easiest way to start exploring shipwrecks. For more information on diving from boats, ask your SSI Dive Center about SSI's Boat Diving Specialty program.

Private Boats

Private boats need a little more discussion. First, the boat, hopefully a good seaworthy craft, needs to be prepared for diving. This includes having all of the safety equipment, communication equipment, navigational equipment, and seamanship experience.

As with wreck diving, duplication is the key to an enjoyable day of boat diving. Many boats choose to have two positioning systems, radios, and depth recorders. Many private boats also utilize tank racks or bungie systems to prevent damage due to tanks rolling in a heavy sea. Since this book is not about seamanship, rescue or metal shop, let's assume that the boat is properly fitted and the operator experienced. For new boat owners, it's recommended to take a course given by the US Power Squadron or Coast Guard Auxiliary.

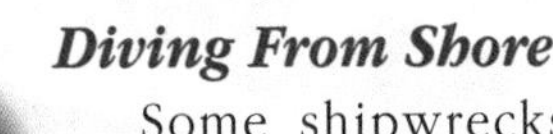

Diving From Shore

Some shipwrecks are located in shallow water close to shore. Navigation on these wrecks involves how to find them and how to get back to shore when the dive is over.

♦ **Bearings.** Whether someone has told you of a wreck or you just stumble into one, it is a good idea to take note of its location so you can return. You can take a bearing by picking at least two objects on the shore at approximately ninety degrees and noting how they line up with objects behind them. For example, a telephone pole lines up with the right side of a house, and a water tower's right side just touches a building's left corner. You will note how accurate these ranges are by swimming a few feet in each direction and noting how each range changes. From now on, all you have to do is to navigate to those ranges, descend, and the wreck should be found again.

- **Compass.** To ensure you will be able to find the site again, take a compass course to your shore entry point and navigate to it. You will need to time your swim back to shore with your watch or dive timer, or you can count your fin kicks. It is easier to navigate to a wreck under water, so you may make a note of what depth you are swimming. Depending on any current and your ability to use a compass accurately, you should swim directly to the wreck. If this fails, you can always surface and use the land bearings before descending again. To learn more about navigation, ask your SSI Dive Center about SSI's *Navigation* Specialty program.

Many shipwrecks located close enough to shore for beach dives are popular for night dives and lobstering. When you surface above the wreck at night, many times the shore line, with all the street and city lights, looks remarkably consistent. The use of a flashing light similar to a road hazard light can vividly mark your exact entry point. This little trick may save a long walk to your car.

Night Diving

Your SSI Dive Center offers the SSI Night and Limited Visibility Diving specialty program to help you hone your skills for diving at night.

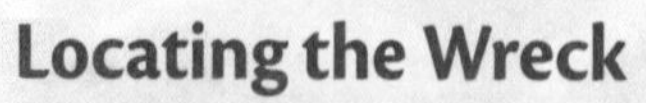

Locating the Wreck

A variety of methods are employed to locate shipwrecks. Increased technological advances, such as side scan sonars and proton magnetometers, have resulted in the discovery of thousands of shipwrecks. Over the years, many of these wrecks have been charted. If you are not interested in searching for undiscovered wrecks, or in diving from charter boats, nautical charts are the best method private boats have to find wrecks.

Charts of Known Wrecks

Most marine supply stores can provide nautical charts with known wreck locations. These charts are a great way to start out. Usually most popular local shipwrecks will be marked on the chart with the site's corresponding Loran numbers. Finding the wreck is usually as simple as navigating to the site, girding the area and then anchoring up, once the wreck's profile is spotted on the graphical depth recorder. Use the largest scale chart available for the area to help make the search easier.

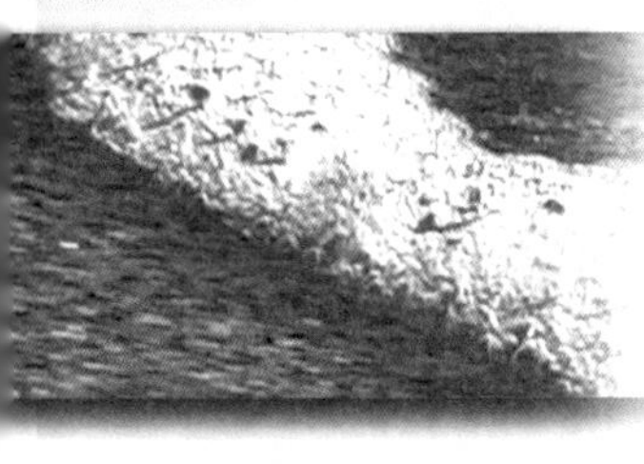

Charts of Unites States waters and its territories are published by the National Oceanic and Atmospheric Administration (NOAA). Nautical charts of foreign waters are published by the U.S. Defense Mapping Agency in Washington D.C., plus many are available from other countries, such as Canada and England.

Charts of U.S. inland waterways and rivers are available from various state agencies or the U.S. Army Corps of Engineers. Your local dive store and instructor may be able to help you locate the nautical charts you need.

Remote Sensing

Finding an undiscovered shipwreck is a dream of all wreck divers. Many wrecks have been located by divers just exploring new areas or checking out new positioning numbers supplied by local fisherman. The method of search is as varied as the type of vessels that sail the sea.

Most successful searches start with a lot of thorough research.

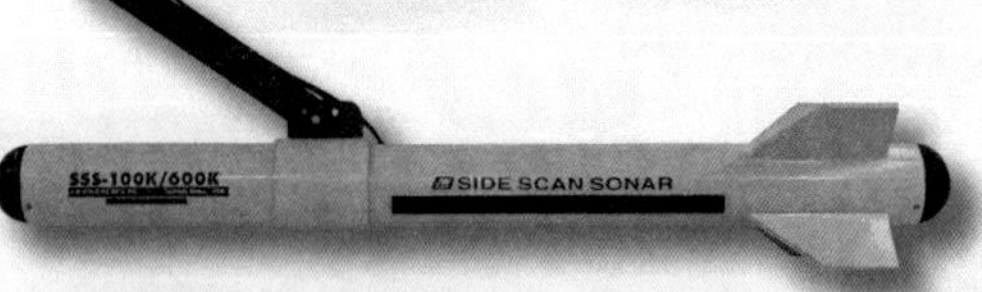

Photo courtesy of J.W. Fishers

Then, when a likely area is derived, the remains can be located with machines such as side scan sonars, proton magnetometers or less expensive equipment like a depth recorder. Other shallow, clear water search methods include towing a diver on a sled while the boat completes a grid of the area. This method is affectionately called, "towing shark bait." Be aware that this method can be dangerous and shouldn't be attempted without some direction and training.

Aerial surveys can also be very helpful, using aircraft, helicopters or even a hot air balloon. Aerial surveys should be done no higher than 500 feet (150 metres). Polarized sunglasses are important, as is a good calm day with little surface chop.

Remember, before buying any expensive equipment or spending days on the boat searching an area, do your homework. Research can narrow the search area down and save countless hours of wasted time.

Also, you must realize that searching for undiscovered wrecks in foreign waters is much more complex than sending away for a chart and using sonar. There are legalities and your safety to consider. Many of these waters are protected, both by the laws and the local people. Before attempting any searches, check with the local dive stores, resorts and law enforcement agencies.

Let's take a look at some of the electronics and machines that are used on boats to help divers locate ship wrecks.

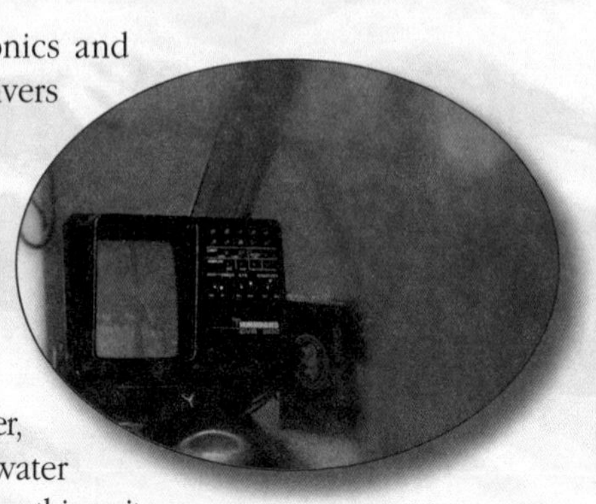

- **Depth Finders.** Depth finders are a basic piece of equipment found on most well equipped dive boats. Recorders can be either paper machines or color monitors. Basically the depth finder, or recorder, graphically draws the depth of water underneath the boat. By monitoring this unit, shipwrecks with high relief can be spotted because the depth becomes immediately shallower. Smaller low-lying wrecks can also be located, but a more experienced eye is needed to watch for depressions and bottom density changes. The combination of depth finder and Loran should be considered mandatory equipment for any wreck search in deep or dark waters.

♦ **Loran C.** Loran, an acronym for Long Range Aid to Navigation, triangulates land-based radio transmission broadcast from approximate right angles and interpolates this information into two lines of numbers. A Loran location is usually exact to within 50 feet (15 metres), which means that each time you return to the exact Loran number where the wreck is, you are within 50 feet of the exact spot. Loran numbers for known shipwrecks are available in a number of shipwreck books as well as on nautical charts. Boaters should realize that the Loran number taken on one boat may be slightly different from the reading observed on another boat. Loran units are often considered indispensable not only for relocating a wreck site but for basic navigation.

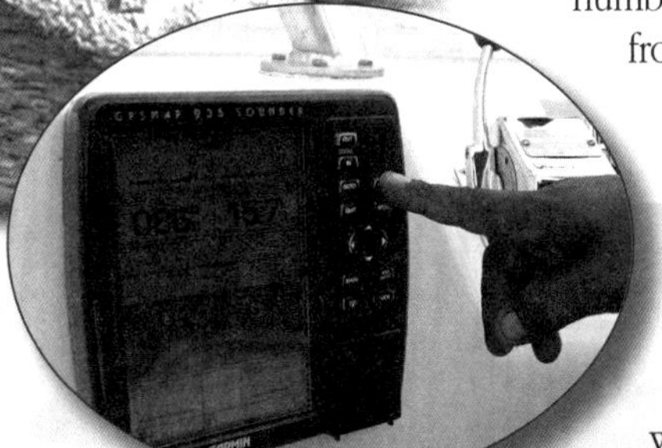

♦ **GPS.** GPS, or Global Positioning System, uses a network of 21 satellites around the world for navigation. No matter where in the world you are, you should be able to pick up at least 5 of these satellites. Only 3 satellites are required to triangulate a position directly to latitude and longitude. This lat-long position is more accurate than the calculated lat-long position given by Loran C. The repeatability of a GPS position, or the ability to go back to the same spot as a shipwreck, is advertised as 330 feet (100 metres) as opposed to 50 feet (15 metres) with Loran, but users claim that it is much more accurate than this, with some units as accurate as 20 feet (6 metres).

DGPS, or Differential GPS, uses both satellites and a land-based station to achieve accuracy to 35 feet (10.5 metres) and is more accurate than Loran. There are very few DGPS stations in operation now, so check with the Coast Guard in your area to see when and where a DGPS station will be established. GPS provides all of the navigation functions as Loran, and is one of the fastest growing navigational systems.

- **Proton Magnetometer.** Proton Magnetometers are passive instruments that record the earth's magnetic field and any disturbances in the field such as large masses of iron. The field disturbance is proportionate to the amount of ferrous iron in the ship. These machines, which also utilize a tow fish, can find any ferrous metals such as cannons, hull plates, and anchors, even when they are buried beneath the ocean floor. This is a sophisticated tool, requiring technical assistance from expert ocean engineers or marine surveyors. Magnetometers are the most often used tool by scientists and treasure hunters for finding shipwrecks.

- **Side Scan Sonar.** Side scan sonar is the most scientific method of locating wrecks. These units are very expensive, so they are not common place in the sport diving community. Basically, most side scan sonars use a tow fish which is towed behind the boat at a determined depth. The sonar relies on the return of sound pulses sent out from the "fish" to map the surface of the sea floor. Any object that is not buried, like a shipwreck, produces echoes which are received by a transducer. The side scan image is like a negative map of what is resting or sitting on top of the sea bed. This information is often computer enhanced to give a detailed image of the wreck. Side scan sonar also requires an experienced operator.

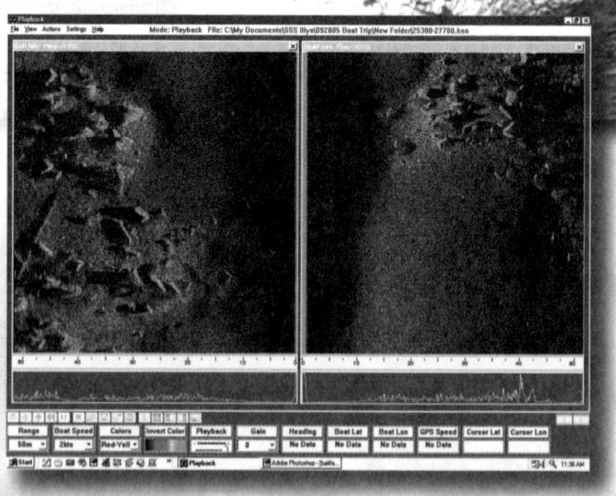

Photo courtesy of J.W. Fishers

Finding the Wreck

Once you get to the wreck's general location, you may still need to find its exact location. In the Caribbean, South

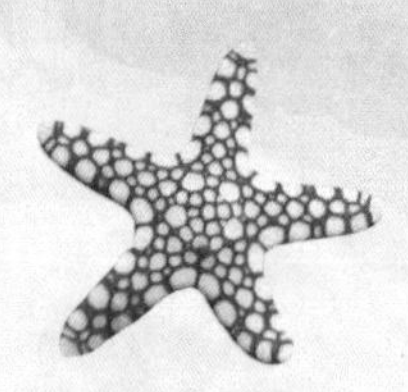

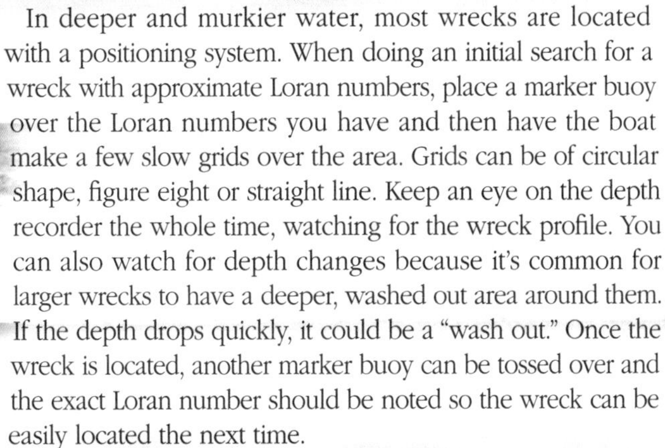

Pacific, or other clear water locations, many wrecks are located with the aid of triangulating land ranges. After aligning these ranges, the skipper looks for uncharacteristic straight lines on the otherwise barren sand or coral bottom.

Remember that mother nature only creates curves. Any straight lines usually indicate a wreck is underneath.

In deeper and murkier water, most wrecks are located with a positioning system. When doing an initial search for a wreck with approximate Loran numbers, place a marker buoy over the Loran numbers you have and then have the boat make a few slow grids over the area. Grids can be of circular shape, figure eight or straight line. Keep an eye on the depth recorder the whole time, watching for the wreck profile. You can also watch for depth changes because it's common for larger wrecks to have a deeper, washed out area around them. If the depth drops quickly, it could be a "wash out." Once the wreck is located, another marker buoy can be tossed over and the exact Loran number should be noted so the wreck can be easily located the next time.

- **Anchoring Procedures.** In deep, murky waters it is customary for boats to anchor with a grapple hook. This procedure is not recommended because it is very damaging to the wrecks. Basically, the grapple drags the bottom until it catches onto a piece of the wreck strong enough to hold it. Unfortunately, it may miss two or three times, stripping off pieces of the wreck until it hooks. Remember, wrecks are not replenishable resources. Once a wreck is destroyed it cannot grow back.

The preferred anchoring procedure is to use a mooring, or to anchor off site, just as you would anchor on a coral reef. This method is more difficult, and requires your bearings to be more precise than when using a grapple hook, but it is also more ecologically sound.

One day, hopefully, the most heavily dived wrecks will have moorings for boats just like our coral reef sites do. In fact, this is a great fund-raising project for your local store or dive club. By raising enough money to set a mooring at your favorite local wreck, you can help extend the life of the wreck.

♦ **Boat Personnel.** When diving from a private boat, there should always be a capable person left in charge of the boat. Never leave the boat unattended while you go diving. Whomever is left topside should be instructed not to allow any other boats to anchor on top of the divers in the water. He/She should also know how to operate the vessel, use a positioning system such as Loran or GPS, have the correct coordinates for the wreck, and know how to use the radio and the proper emergency channels.

Summary

While many great wrecks lie close enough to shore for beach dives, many wrecks require a boat to get to them. Charter boats are the best choice for divers that simply want to dive a known wreck, without having to worry about locating and anchoring over the site. Should you choose to dive from a private vessel, you will need to choose a method, or methods for locating the wreck site.

For known wrecks, it's likely that you will be able to purchase a marked nautical chart of the region that wreck is located in. However, for uncharted wrecks you will need to complete thorough research, and create a solid plan before you go hunting for your wreck. Remember, your SSI Dive Center is a great resource to consult with when starting your wreck diving career, whether to dive known wrecks, or to start an adventure finding new ones.

In the next section we will discuss proper planning, the procedures for exploring wrecks, potential hazards when wreck diving and how to avoid them.

Section 3 Review Questions

1. The easiest way to dive a shipwreck is to sign on to a

   ________________________________.

2. You can take a bearing by picking at least two objects on the shore at approximately ninety degrees and noting how they ________

   ________________________________.

3. Most marine supply stores can provide nautical charts with known

   ______________________.

4. Loran-C triangulates land-based radio transmissions broadcast from approximate right angles and interpolates this information into

   ____

   ____________.

5. When doing an initial search for a wreck with approximate Loran numbers, place a marker buoy over the Loran numbers you have, and then have the boat make ________________________

   ________________________________.

6. The preferred anchoring procedure is to use a mooring, or to anchor off site, just as you would anchor ____________

   ______________________.

Diving the Wreck

Section 4 Objectives

After completing this section you will be able to:

- Describe how to properly plan your wreck dive,
- Understand proper procedures for exploring wrecks,
- Describe possible hazards when wreck diving, and how to avoid them,
- Understand the proper surface and exit procedures following a wreck dive.

Once the shipwreck is located it's time to suit up, jump in and go diving. Before descending, however, it's important for dive partners to discuss and agree on a dive plan, objectives, conditions, and depth and time parameters.

Good communication between buddies prior to the dive will help make the dive safer and more enjoyable for everyone.

Planning the Dive

Before entering the water you will need to discuss and plan out your dive with your buddy. You will also need to check out all your scuba equipment to be sure it's all in proper working order. Be sure to discuss specific details about the dive. You need to both agree not only on an objective, but also on exact parameters for each. Discuss the details such as who will hold the tether reel, who will lead and who will follow. The follower should always stay in the same position relative to the leader. For example, on the leader's right side. This way the lead diver does not constantly have to turn 360 degrees to spot his partner. Plan a no-decompression dive for the planned maximum depth by referring to your computer or the dive tables, discuss alternative dive plans and objectives if conditions on the bottom are not agreeable to the dive plan, as well as what action to take should some sort of emergency occur on the dive.

Personal Limits and Responsibilities

It is very important to realize and understand that each diver has different skill, comfort and experience levels.

Never plan a dive beyond the limits of your personal comfort and ability.

Compatibility

It's not hard to understand that a diver who wants to photograph the wreck would not be a good dive partner for someone who plans to go lobstering.

Be aware of peer pressure and the stress it can create in diving It is up to you to communicate your own personal diving limits to your buddy, to the other members of the team, and to the diving leader.

It is your responsibility as a wreck diver to judge whether or not your skill level and equipment are adequate for the level of difficulty the wreck poses. This good judgement will allow you to be a responsible and competent wreck diver.

Goals

Most wreck divers have specific goals for each dive. These goals can vary from simple exploration, lobstering and fish watching to photography, videography or archaeology. It's quite important for dive partners to agree on a primary goal.

Depth and Time Parameters

The next step to planning a dive on any wreck site is to find out how deep the wreck is. Once the depth is determined the dive team should plan their dive around the no-decompression limits. This means to check the dive tables to determine how long you will stay. Decide on a maximum depth your team will descend to. Remember that many shipwrecks are three dimensional so even if the wreck sits in 100 feet (30 metres), the top of the wreck may sit as shallow as 60 feet (18 metres). This means that it may be quite possible for divers to spend their entire dive without dropping below 60 or 70 feet (21 metres).

Since most wreck dives are made off dive boats and most divers choose to descend and ascend on the dive boat's anchor line, you will also need to plan at what time you will stop exploring and start returning to the anchor line. Remember to plan the dive and dive the plan.

Currents and Surge

Depending on the condition and location of each shipwreck, currents and surge can have an adverse effect on dive safety. If the current is too strong or the surge too powerful it may be necessary to terminate the dive. Most times divers need only be aware of these conditions. For example, if there is a mild tidal current it is advisable to swim into the current as you explore the site. This way, after you turn around and return to the anchor line you will not have to fight against the current.

Surge, on the other hand, can be a little more unnerving. At times, even in deep water, surge created by surface waves can lift a diver off the bottom then push or pull him/her off the wreck. Water movement caused by the surge can also cause periodic suction through restricted areas and tight spaces such as hatches.

Shipwrecks often have jagged, sharp edges and heavy surge can be dangerous.

Visibility

Visibility is another key factor to enjoying and safely participating in the sport of recreational shipwreck diving. Often conditions on the bottom are hard to predict so divers should have contingency plans. In good visibility, shipwrecks are easy to explore and find your way around on, but if you descend to find somewhat cloudy visibility the dive isn't necessarily ruined. Proper planning and equipment comes into play in these conditions. A tether line is a navigational tool that allows exploration in poor visibility.

Divers often report enjoying slightly dark or murky conditions. It seems that poor visibility can force divers to concentrate more on what's directly in front of them rather than looking at the larger images that can be observed on clear water days. Nevertheless, in clear or murky water, dive teams should plan and be prepared to cope with the conditions they encounter as they descend.

Nature of the Wreck

In addition to the water conditions, the diver should take into consideration the nature of the wreck itself, and plan for any possible problems.

- Is the wreck known to contain sharp or jagged edges?
- Are there cables, nets or other entanglement hazards?
- Do doors and hatches pose a threat of entrapment?

The hazards on some wrecks are often hidden beneath the growth of marine life or in limited visibility. Extreme caution is the best prevention, but a little research will also help. If you are not diving with an organized charter boat that can provide this type of information, you should seek it out from a local dive store, instructor or club before diving the site.

Lost Buddy Procedure

Storms, accidents, and lost divers are some of the problems that could require buddies to regroup and address the situation. During the formation of the pre-dive plan, divers should be briefed on the emergency call back procedure. Some boat operators have an emergency recall system which is basically an underwater siren on the dive boat. Other operators use a flag system.

Pre-Plan

You and your buddy should establish a lost buddy procedure should you become separated. You should discuss how long you will look for each other under water, and when to go get help.

KNOWLEDGE SKILLS EQUIPMENT EXPERIENCE DIVER DIAMOND SSI SCUBA SCHOOLS INTERNATIONAL

Go, No-Go Diving Decision

Never let peer pressure lead you into making a dive beyond your own capabilities or the initial dive plan. The rule is "If you have any doubt, don't do it." Many highly trained and qualified divers have sat on the boat when they just didn't feel right about the diving conditions, the location, or their buddies. As a rule, try to remain calm no matter what situation arises; remaining calm and in control is mandatory. Staying in control helps to avoid panic and ensure proper air consumption.

Dealing with stress is much easier on the surface, before the dive begins. A wreck diver must be disciplined and know when to make the correct go, no-go diving decision, as well as when it is time to terminate a dive that may become dangerous.

Remember, the final responsibility for making the decision whether or not to dive rests with you. There is always another dive, and another diving day if you make the proper diving decisions.

Exploring the Wreck

The thrill and excitement of exploration is probably what makes shipwreck diving such a popular sport. Each dive brings a new adventure. Whether you are exploring a German U-Boat or sunken luxury liner, shipwreck diving is an experience that our land-locked counterparts may never truly appreciate. Only through the sport of scuba diving can we glide effortlessly through the sunken remains of vessels spanning centuries of maritime history. Exploration of new sites can lead to the discovery of previously unknown shipwrecks. Whether examining artifacts from a freight steamer or taking photographs of a vessel's helm, exploration has always played a key role in shipwreck diving.

Descent Procedures

Use the method of entry that is best for the diving conditions. If you are diving from a boat, your captain will explain the entry procedure.

It is recommended to use a line for descent. These lines could include a current line, which attaches from the stern of the boat to the anchor line, or you may use a separate descent line. Lines make it easier to control your descent, clear your ears and handle extra equipment such as a camera. Lines also allow you to descend in a more head-first position. Feet-first descents can damage the wreck and stir up excess silt. When wreck diving in limited visibility, the anchor line will also lead you directly to the wreck site.

While descent lines are the preferred method, free descents are also valid. In clear water, for example, you can most likely see the wreck and will find it without difficulty. On a free descent, you and your buddy should try to descend at the same pace. Maintain visual contact and watch below as you descend to avoid "crash landing" into the reef or wreck.

Navigation

Most wreck dives are done from a boat, anchored above the site. Depending on visibility and currents, it can be difficult at times to find the anchor line when it is time to surface. Not returning to the anchor line could mean a long surface swim back to the boat or a free-floating safety or decompression stop. Here are a few helpful hints for navigating around a wreck.

- **Current.** First, as with any boat dive, divers should try to start their dive into the current; this will make for an easier swim when returning. If the wreck is intact and the visibility is good, it is often no problem to note where you are and return later. If you cannot locate the anchor line you should surface up current which permits you to ride with the current back to the dive boat.

- **Perimeter Search.** A common navigational method is the perimeter search. With this method the anchor is located near the wreck so the diver can descend down the anchor line and then swim directly to either side of the wreck. The next step is to take note of a unique feature, characteristic or landmark and its relative position to you as you swim down the wreck. When you want to return, simply turn around and swim back along the wreck's perimeter until you see the same object or landmark. When it comes time to ascend, swim towards the centre of the wreckage where you should be able to find the anchor line or ascent line.

- **Tether Line Reel.** If visibility is limited, or if the wreck is scattered over a large area with no distinct reference points, divers can use a tether line reel, clipping one end on or near the anchor while letting line out as they explore the wreckage. This navigation method is almost foolproof because as long as the line is not severed, you can easily return to your starting point. Although this method is dependable, it does have its disadvantages. It limits a diver's investigation to the length of the line, and the same territory must be covered during the second half of the dive.

- **Cross-Wreck Line.** Another line that is helpful in poor visibility is the cross-wreck line. This line can be either a temporary or permanent line that runs across the wreck, or across a scattered, broken up wreck. This line works much like the tether line except it is not attached to you with a reel. The diver can work his/her way across the line in very poor visibility, or h/shee can make short explorations from the line, using it as the known heading that leads back to the anchor line.

- **Strobe Lights.** Other methods include attaching a small strobe light to the anchor line about 20 or 30 feet (6 to 9 metres) off the bottom. Divers can then freely explore the wreck as long as they remain in site of the strobe light.

♦ **Compass.** While compasses can be valuable navigation tools under water, you must be aware that the steel and iron present in wrecks can affect your compass reading by attracting the compass needle.

Do not expect your compass to be accurate as it normally would be when navigating on a wreck.

In addition, a compass is not very helpful unless you know how to properly use it. Before using a compass on wreck dives, you should consider taking an SSI Navigation Specialty program offered by your SSI Dive Center.

Silt and suspended particles are a concern to divers who explore wrecks. Silt can be raised by one fin kick, and even a diver's bubbles can loosen fine sediment and rust. The end result is reduced visibility, sometimes to the point of zero visibility. Extra care should be used to avoid stirring up sediment because a total loss of visibility can be very stressful. If you have taken special navigational precautions, such as noting landmarks, swimming into the current, or using a tether line, you should be able to navigate back to the ascent line. If you relax and let the sediment settle, your visibility may increase.

After a while navigation becomes second nature; the more dives you make, the better you become. Also, as you make more dives on a particular wreck you will begin to memorize the wreck's layout. Pretty soon you will recognize parts of the ship and their location in relationship to other areas of the wreck. After many excursions to the same wreck, you will be able to navigate simply from your own knowledge of the area.

Communication

Underwater communication is discussed in every basic diver's manual and in all certification classes. Everyone should remember the basic hand signals and what they stand for (refer to your SSI Open Water Diver manual to review basic hand signals). In clear water situations these signals may work fine, but if the wreck is located in limited visibility, hand signals and slates become very hard to use.

For example, if two divers are using a tether line and the lead diver has the reel in his/her right hand and a light in his left hand, how can he communicate with his buddy? To use hand signals, he/she would have to put down the light or let go of the line reel. If the light was put down, neither diver would be able to see the hand signals, and putting the reel down is not a good idea. This attempt to communicate may cause the divers to stop, sink to the bottom and stir up silt, thus ruining the visibility.

Let's look at two other options for communicating on wrecks.

- **Voice Communication.** An alternative is to communicate by talking to each other while diving. There is no trick or special equipment needed, just stay close to each other and talk very slowly into your second-stage regulator. Keep the sentences short, like, "let's go up," or "how much air?" In fact, when you first start, try communicating in one syllable words like "up" or "air." If you dive with the same person often enough, you will quickly start to understand each other. The real benefit of this method can be appreciated when diving at night or in limited visibility. Go back to the original scenario: Both divers could talk to each other while continuing to explore the wreck; they didn't have to stop or put down any of their equipment. It takes a little practice, but it's worth it. Of course, if your message is not understood it should still be written down or communicated through hand signals. Convenience is not worth the risk of miscommunication.

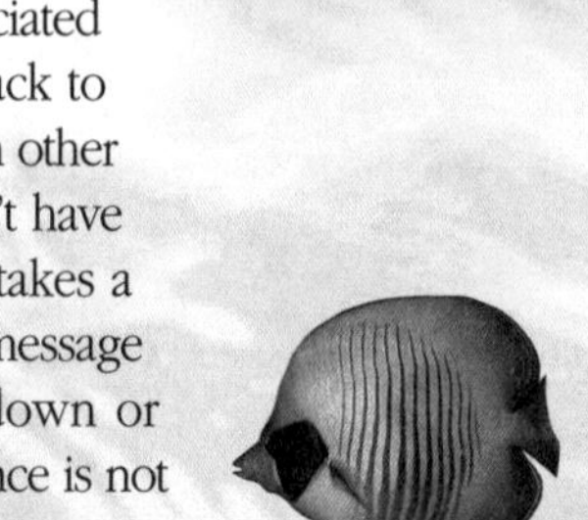

- **Line Pulls.** Another way to communicate is with line pulls. If you and your buddy are using a tether line reel or a buddy line you can communicate by pulling on the line. For example, you can devise a set of signals to communicate basic messages, such as one pull on the line means "stop," two pulls on the line means "come here," and three pulls means "help, emergency!"

Mental Attitude

Wreck divers should use some of the rules cave divers have been using with much success for years.

If any diver in the team does not feel comfortable with a dive, then that dive should be immediately terminated.

Staying calm, moving slowly and knowing your equipment can all help to prevent stress. Preventing stress can also come from diving frequently, not being over weighted, making sure all of your equipment operates correctly and familiarizing yourself with the wreck.

Other Interests

If you are interested in learning more about stress and diving, you should look into taking SSI's Diver Stress & Rescue program from your local SSI Dive Center.

The proper, positive mental attitude is very important when participating in any wreck dive. If an improperly trained diver were to penetrate a wreck, encountering darkness and stirred up silt, claustrophobia and stress could soon lead to panic. If this situation is not immediately handled with a cool head, the results could be fatal. This is why penetrating wrecks is not recommended by SSI, unless you have plenty of experience, additional training and the proper equipment.

Ascent Procedures

As with descents, it is recommended that you use a line to ascend to the surface. This line could be the anchor line, a separate ascent line, or an up-line. Using an up-line for ascents is discussed in more detail in Section 2, Wreck Diving Equipment.

A line allows you to control your rate of ascent, handle extra equipment, and stay with your buddy. A line also allows you to make a safety stop at 15 feet (5 metres) for 3 to 5 minutes.

This safety stop is recommended on all dives, not just deep dives.

Remember, should you have a problem on ascent, ditch any extra equipment in your hands, such as lights or cameras. This will allow you to handle yourself in an emergency. At the end of the dive, you may also become tired or in danger due to the excess drag of this equipment. Should you need immediate positive buoyancy on ascent or on the surface, you should ditch your weight belt and make an emergency buoyant ascent to the surface.

Hazards

While wreck diving is known to have some hazards, most are avoidable. All divers should know how to react if, and when, they do encounter these situations. Entanglement, entrapment and disorientation are three of the more common hazards that a wreck diver might encounter. Remember, during any stressful situation the rule is: Stop, Breathe, Think and then Act!

STOP BREATHE THINK ACT

- **Entanglement.** While it is certainly not something that divers should stay up at night worrying about, entanglement is definitely a valid concern that is best avoided. Because shipwrecks attract fish, they also attract fishermen; therefore, they are often draped in monofilament line, fish nets and lost anchor lines. Even the tether line reels that wreck divers carry can cause entanglement when they are not used properly. Although many Caribbean shipwrecks do not have this problem, when diving in coastal waters or in many inland waterways, divers have to be aware of this hazard.

The best way to deal with these hazards is to avoid them. Wreck divers should always be alert to their surroundings, and should streamline their dive equipment so that it is less likely to create a snag. If, however, entanglement does occur divers should be prepared to handle the situation. Again, the basic rule is the same: Stop, Breathe, Think and then Act. Stopping all motion will prevent further entanglement until you can free yourself.

When divers get snagged in monofilament line, they should be able to take out one of their two diver's tools (always kept sharp) and cut the line. This type of snag should cause little or no stress since it should become very routine for divers to break or cut the monofilament.

Fish nets are less common and usually much easier to avoid. These nets are often easily observed. However, in dark or murky waters, these nets can be very hazardous.

If your buddy is close by he or she can assist. However, a dive buddy should not be completely relied upon. The purpose of the buddy system is not for one diver to be strong and make up for his partner's weakness. Rather, every wreck diver should be properly equipped and experienced. Each should carry a main diver's tool and at least one additional back-up. The blades should be kept razor sharp to quickly cut through any rope or line that may entangle a diver.

♦ **Entrapment.** Entrapment inside a wreck is an extreme hazard. This can happen when a diver tries to fit through a hole that is not large enough, somehow gets lost inside the wreckage or if a piece of wreckage accidentally comes loose and traps the diver. This is one of the worst hazards of wreck diving and requires absolute control: both physically and mentally. Again: Stop, Breathe, Think and then Act.

Struggling usually only results in quicker air consumption. If you are stuck, stay calm and try to free yourself or signal your buddy to assist you.

If you're lost inside the wreck, try turning off all lights and then look for any ambient light which may lead to an opening large enough to fit through. If your predicament is caused by kicked up sediment and you're at the beginning or middle of your dive, try staying motionless for about one minute. The silt may settle enough to see your way out, but be forewarned that one minute may seem like an eternity. Calm, collective thought and breath control is the key to dealing with any hazardous situation and maximizing your air supply.

Of course, proper wreck diving skills teach us not to depend on memory alone to find our way out of a shipwreck. The proper use of a tether line reel provides the accurate exit route.

- **Disorientation.** At times it can be quite easy to get disoriented when diving on shipwrecks. Disorientation is most hazardous when penetrating into a wreck's interior. Silt gets kicked up and divers can very easily get lost.

Unless you have advanced wreck diving training, extensive experience, and the proper equipment it is strongly recommended that you avoid penetrating a wreck's interior.

Disorientation can also occur on the exterior of wrecks and even under the best of conditions. For example, a diver could easily swim along the wrong side of the wreck ending up in her stern when the anchor is in her bow. For this type of disorientation divers must rely on their scuba skills. If your bottom time is up or you are running low on air it's time to head up.

Use a lift bag and reel to create an up line, if you have one, or just control your buoyancy to make a free ascent.

If you still have air and bottom time try to re-orientate yourself as to your position and navigate back to the anchor. Remember the key to working through any hazardous situation is to stay calm and not panic. Remember: Stop, Breathe, Think and then Act.

♦ **Marine Life.** Many wrecks are covered with a vast array of marine life, including some that can cause harm. Typically, most divers will be injured by animals that puncture, not bite. These animals include the urchin and the barnacle, both of which can cover wrecks. To prevent a puncture wound, wear gloves and an exposure suit at all times and, of course, be careful. Remember, however, that divers can also harm marine life. Be careful to avoid damaging the marine life on wrecks, just as you protect the coral reels.

♦ **Penetration.** A penetration dive can be defined as a dive in which the diver does not have clear, unrestricted access to the surface at all times. Penetration is an advanced form of wreck diving, and is beyond the scope of recreational wreck diving and this course. Penetration should only be attempted by divers with adequate experience, training and equipment. Good judgment should be used before entering into any overhead environment.

More information on penetration can be found in Section 5, Advanced Wreck Diving.

Wrapping Up the Dive

No dive is over until you are out of the water. Safe exiting and surface procedures should be followed, especially if you are carrying additional equipment such as goodie bags and cameras. Once you are out of the water you should wrap up the dive by completing your DiveLog and taking care of your equipment.

Surface and Exit Procedures

Once you surface, you should inflate your BC immediately until you achieve positive buoyancy. If you are tired, cold, or carrying a lot of equipment you may want to ask your buddy for help. If you are diving from a boat, the surface personnel can toss you a line or float to help you back to the boat.

Always hand up any object you are carrying before you climb a boat ladder. Your captain will advise you of any special exiting procedures. Remember, keep your mask, BC and second-stage regulator in place so that you can see, breathe and float until you are out of the water.

You can also drop a special down line near the anchor line. This line is useful for hooking on your extra equipment or goody bags so they can be hoisted onto the boat after you exit. This can make exiting at night, in high seas, or in poor weather easier because you do not have to worry about the excess weight and drag caused by this extra equipment.

Logging the Dive

Evaluations of each dive and documentation of observations can increase the success and enjoyment of future wreck dives. Your SSI DiveLog is the most practical place to store this information. You can use the back of your DiveLog page to record maps or observations, and if more space is needed, you can add one of the SSI Lined Log Pages. These pages are nothing more than additional pages for narrative. These, and all DiveLog refill packs, can be purchased through your SSI Dive Center.

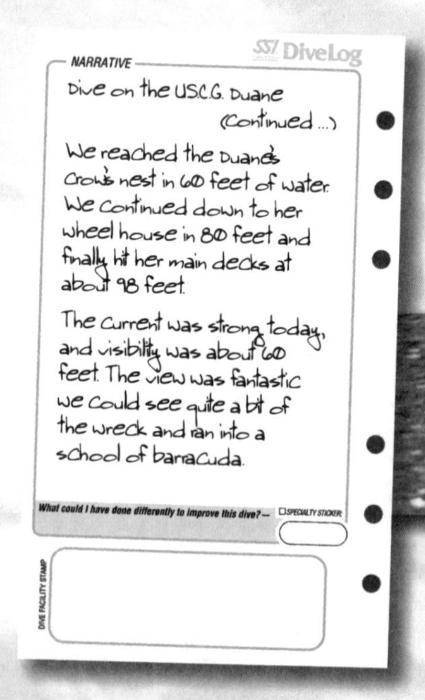

Remember, another good reason to log your dives is that every dive counts toward your SSI levels of certification. Whether you are working toward your Advanced Open Water Diver, Master Diver, Century Diver or even your Platinum Pro5000 Diver rating, every logged dive counts!

Equipment Care and Maintenance

Because wreck diving is a demanding activity, you should learn to take extra care of your equipment. Properly maintained equipment will last for many years, and will cause fewer problems during your dive.

Proper maintenance includes washing, drying and storing your equipment according to manufacturers instructions. It also includes having your equipment serviced at least on an annual basis.

Your equipment is a big investment, by caring for it you can prevent loss, damage, and premature replacement. For more information on care and maintenance of scuba equipment, ask your instructor about SSI's Equipment Techniques Specialty program.

Summary

When diving in other situations we follow the guideline "never plan a dive beyond the limits of your personal comfort and ability." This adage is equally, if not more important to follow when wreck diving.

When planning with your buddy, be sure to discuss the goal(s) of your dive, depth and dive time parameters, and the conditions on the wreck. Don't forget to discuss the lost buddy procedure that should be followed in the event you lose track of each other during the dive. Also, reinforce that anyone at anytime can abort the dive for any reason.

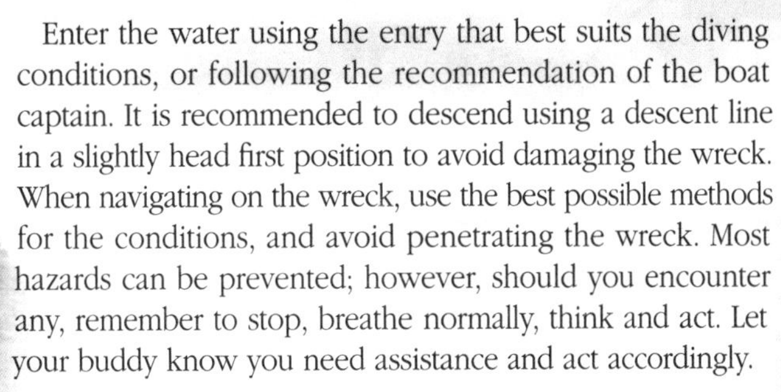

Enter the water using the entry that best suits the diving conditions, or following the recommendation of the boat captain. It is recommended to descend using a descent line in a slightly head first position to avoid damaging the wreck. When navigating on the wreck, use the best possible methods for the conditions, and avoid penetrating the wreck. Most hazards can be prevented; however, should you encounter any, remember to stop, breathe normally, think and act. Let your buddy know you need assistance and act accordingly.

As with your descent, it is recommended to use a line for your ascent. This will help you:

- Control your ascent rate,
- Stay with your buddy,
- Handle any extra equipment,
- Complete your safety stop at 15 feet (5 metres) for 3 to 5 minutes.

Once you're out of the water, log the dive and take care of your equipment.

In the next section we will discuss how other SSI specialty skills can add to your enjoyment of wreck diving and why wreck penetration should only be planned and executed by trained, experienced wreck divers.

Section 4 Review Questions

1. It is your responsibility as a wreck diver to judge whether or not your skill level and equipment are adequate for the ____.

2. If there is a mild tidal current it is advisable to swim into the current as you explore the site. This way, after you turn around and return to the anchor line you will not have to ________________________________.

3. A tether line is a navigational tool that allows exploration ____________________.

4. The final responsibility for making the decision whether or not to dive ____________________.

5. Lines allow you to descend in a more head-first position. Feet-first descents can damage the wreck and ________________________________.

6. Be aware that the steel and iron present in wrecks can affect your compass reading by ________________________________.

7. If you and your buddy are using a tether line reel or a buddy line you can communicate by ________________________________.

8. ______________, ______________ and ______________ are three of the more common hazards a wreck diver might encounter.

9. Typically, most divers will be injured by animals that ____________________, not bite.

10. A penetration dive can be defined as a dive in which the diver does not have ____ ____________________ at all times.

Advanced Wreck Diving

Section 5 Objectives

After completing this section you will understand:

- How other specialty skills can add enjoyment to wreck diving,
- The definition of "Wreck Penetration,"
- Why wreck penetration should only be planned and executed by trained, experienced veteran wreck divers,
- That this course is not intended to train divers to execute wreck penetration dives.

Just as snow skiers start out on the beginner trails and work their way to the more experienced slopes, wreck divers serve their apprenticeship while diving shallower wrecks. Once the art of wreck diving is mastered their is no limitation as to the types and diversification of advanced activities to be applied to wreck diving. Advanced training and experience permits exploration of deeper wrecks, photography, videography, and archaeology to name a few.

Divers can also utilize other specialty skills like navigation and night diving to better enhance their wreck diving experiences.

Deep Diving

Shipwrecks lying in water deeper than 60 feet (18 metres) are considered deep wrecks. Divers wishing to explore these sites must employ all the specific wreck diving skills needed for the type of wreck and diving

conditions, while also dealing with the increased effects of pressure. Some of the dangers of deep diving include nitrogen narcosis and decompression sickness.

Deep dives involve additional planning to ensure you stay within the no-decompression limits, plus you need an understanding of what to do should you enter decompression status. Even though some of the additional equipment and back-up systems that are necessary for deep diving are covered in this manual, it is highly recommended that you take an SSI Deep Diving Specialty program before participating in any dive beyond 100 feet (30 metres).

Night Diving

We have spent some time discussing limited visibility diving and the precautions you must take when diving, because many wrecks are located in limited visibility. Night diving, however, poses a few additional hazards that should be addressed.

A wreck that is easy to locate and navigate during the day, suddenly becomes new and strange at night. While the dark waters of the night bring out some amazing colors and marine life, your visibility suddenly becomes limited to the power of your light source. It is much easier to become disoriented at night, making it more important to have good navigation skills. Communication, planning, safety lines and back-up equipment also become more critical at night than they were during the day.

While there is some special equipment involved with night diving, we have addressed the use of lights and back-up lights in Section 2. However, due to the many new challenges involved with night diving, it is recommended that you take a Night/Limited Visibility Diving Specialty program at your SSI Dive Center before participating in any night dives.

Photography

Taking photographs under water has fascinated divers for years. With a little luck and a lot of skill, a diver can bring home the beauty of the undersea world for all to enjoy. Wreck photography is just a little more demanding than fish or reef photos, but it's a lot more rewarding.

The challenge involved with mixing wreck diving and photography is that the diver must be able to operate both wreck diving equipment and camera equipment simultaneously. In addition, wrecks offer other challenges such as deep, cold water, and limited visibility conditions.

One recommendation is that you do not take up photography until you have some dive experience and good buoyancy control under your belt.

Your wreck diving skills such as hovering effortlessly, checking your air, time, depth and anchor location should be second nature before adding an additional skill such as photography.

Once you commit to the task of taking underwater images, you are really taking on an underwater job, but the satisfaction of producing a fine picture quickly diminishes the memory of all the challenges that preceded its making. The best way to learn about photography is the same way you learned about wreck diving, by taking an SSI Digital Underwater Photography Specialty program.

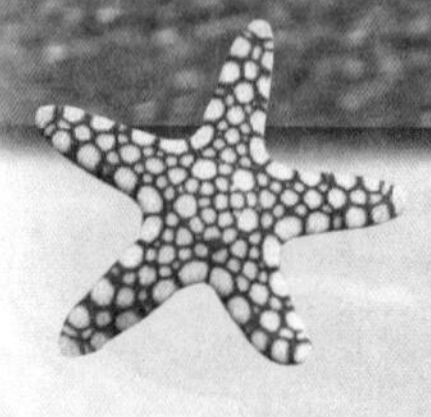

Before diving into a wreck with a camera in hand, streamline yourself even more than normal. You may want to leave your extra tools and goodie bag on the boat since it's hard to do it all. In regard to air supply for deep wrecks, many photographers opt for double cylinders with a single second-stage regulator and pony. Given the complexity of underwater photography, this setup eliminates the need to switch air sources while under water.

When taking wreck photos use a wide angle lens so you can capture maximum wreckage while staying as close to the subject as possible. A powerful, wide angle strobe is also essential. Wreck photography is usually a battle against the lack of light.

To deal with the darkness inside a wreck and to avoid fumbling around with a light in one hand and a camera in the other, many serious photographers mount a dive light to their camera system. Others wear head or helmet mounted dive lights or mount a small modeling light onto the strobe.

Dealing with the always present silt and sediment around shipwrecks can be solved with speed. Wreck photographers don't have the luxury of spending five minutes setting up for the shot or making a camera adjustment to bracket each shot. They have to shoot the picture before any silt gets disturbed. Suspended particles will ruin a photo opportunity. Since time is of the essence, wreck divers must learn to bracket their photographs by taking a series of shots as they approach the intended subject. This is done without changing any camera or strobe settings. Another method is to hand hold the strobe off the camera. This lets the photographer bracket the exposure by moving the strobe closer or further from the subject while positioning the strobe to reduce incidental illumination and back scatter.

Shipwrecks offer the underwater photographer an endless amount of photo opportunities. Whether you're photographing a porthole, fish, lobster or any of the other majestic photo opportunities that shipwrecks offer, divers will almost certainly never run out of interesting subjects.

Videography

Shooting underwater video is a lot easier than successful still photography. Video is often used by wreck divers and archaeologists when creating sketches of a site. Video quickly and somewhat inexpensively captures all of the wreck's details and is available for review immediately after the dive. By using either ambient light or video lights divers can easily capture their entire dive on video. Of course, many of the same skills and techniques are used, but video is a more forgiving medium. Many systems are point and shoot with no need to focus and light balance each scene. Certainly the most popular format is Mini-DV. The main reason is size and quality. Mini-DV cameras and tapes are small and compact while providing extended battery and tape life. There are also any new recording methods and resolutions available for capturing your video. Consult your SSI Dealer for more information.

Underwater Archaeology

Underwater archaeology evolved from the early interests of scholars such as the monks of Lochness. Over the centuries scholars, treasure hunters, fishermen, and recreational divers have helped locate most known wrecks and have both explored, and exploited, these fragile resources. Underwater archaeology allows us to maximize the information contained within these historic shipwrecks. By adhering to archaeological methods we can learn much about ancient shipbuilding methods and even the lifestyles of the early marine travelers. Of course, it's impossible for marine archaeologists to survey all known shipwrecks. It also serves no purpose since many of the wrecks that sport divers explore are contemporary and offer no hidden secrets into the past. It is however, important that recreational divers respect the significance of historical shipwrecks.

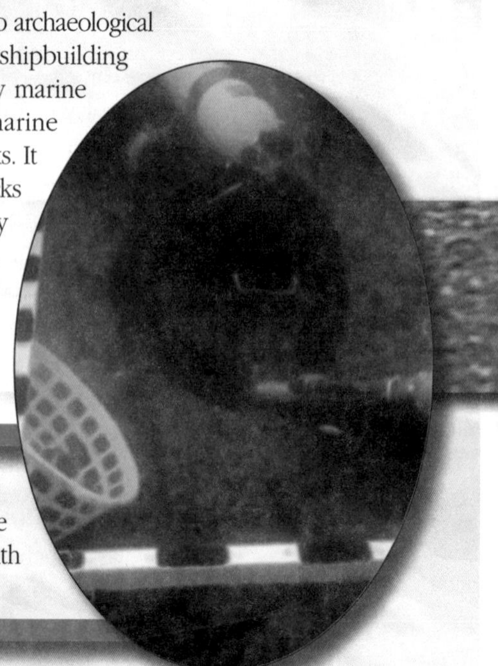

To reiterate, divers should take nothing but photographs and leave nothing but bubbles on any wreck with historic significance.

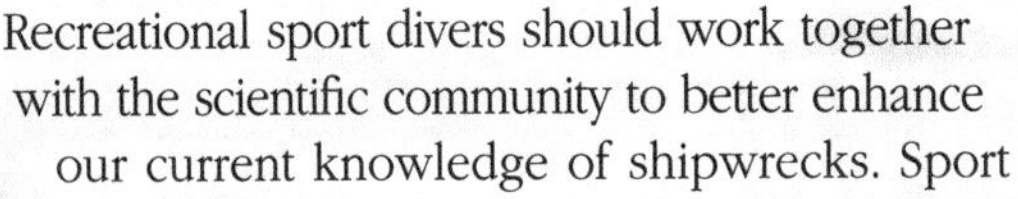

Recreational sport divers should work together with the scientific community to better enhance our current knowledge of shipwrecks. Sport divers have the ability and numbers to provide invaluable service, while scientists have the proper skills, techniques and equipment needed to accurately survey each site. Cooperation and education on both sides will ensure the future of recreational wreck diving and the advancement of underwater archaeology.

If you or your dive club are interested in learning more about archaeology, or are interested in donating your time to help survey one of your local wrecks you should contact your state archaeologist for help. Begin by contacting the State Historic Preservation Office. This office can put you in contact with the person in charge of underwater wrecks and resources. The state archaeologist is a valuable resource to either help you get started in surveying the site, or to put you in contact with universities or museums who are in need of divers for surveying purposes. Archaeology is a great way to learn more about wrecks, plus it is an exciting activity for divers who are looking for a new outlet for their diving.

Search and Recovery

Artifact collection has been a popular aspect of wreck diving since the inception of the sport. Many divers have found treasures ranging from brass portholes and china, to ancient weaponry. However, today's divers must consider the laws and ethics regarding artifact collection.

In some areas, artifact collection is a serious criminal offense. Boats have been impounded and divers arrested for violating restrictions intended to preserve the integrity of the wreck. The simple fact that once an object is taken it cannot be enjoyed by others, may give reason to reconsider removing artifacts from a wreck site.

Wreck divers should consult with local dive stores and authorities before removing artifacts from a wreck site. Artifact collection is strictly controlled, just as the collection of corals or other marine life is, and is against the law in every state in the U.S. without a permit.

If you are diving from a charter boat, your captain will most likely have a policy regarding collection of artifacts. This policy may be based as much upon personal opinion as law. As a wreck diver, you too will have to make a personal choice about recovering artifacts.

If you are interested in finding out more about search and recovery techniques, you should look into an SSI Search and Recovery Specialty program at your local SSI Authorized Dive Center. This course covers mapping and lift bag techniques.

Wreck Penetration

WARNING

Wreck penetration can lead to serious injury or even death. Some wreck divers explore the interiors of certain wrecks. Penetration of wrecks, however, should only be executed by very experienced, veteran wreck divers, if at all. The penetration of ANY wreck by the novice is inadvisable. When divers penetrate wrecks, they are doing so at their own risk. Wreck penetration is beyond the scope of this program.

Summary

Wreck diving offers the diver a unique and diverse diving experience, unlike the natural habitats of the kelp forests and coral reefs. Wrecks offer an intriguing view of the past, a glimpse of civilizations that can only be experienced by the wreck diver.

Wreck diving is a skill that can enhance a lifetime of underwater experiences. The possibilities are virtually unlimited with new wrecks being discovered or sunk as artificial reefs every year. The pursuit of more challenging wrecks is a natural progression for the avid diver. However, no amount of experience in wreck diving, or any other specialty, for that matter, should preclude a constant awareness of safety.

Safe wreck diving all comes down to judgement. The responsible wreck diver learns to judge whether his own personal comfort limits and skills qualify him to participate in a particular wreck dive. Because being a certified wreck diver does not qualify you to dive every wreck, it only gives you the license to begin to learn about the many challenges and experiences that wreck diving offers.

Section 5 Review Questions

1. Shipwrecks lying in water deeper than __________ are considered deep wrecks.

2. It is much easier to become disoriented at night, making it more important to have good ______________________________ __________________.

3. The challenge involved with mixing wreck diving and photography is that the diver must be able to operate both __________________ __________________ and ______________________________ simultaneously.

4. Video quickly and inexpensively captures all of the wreck's details and is available ______________________________ __________________.

5. Whether the wreck is in freshwater or salt water, these structures provide a habitat for a wide range of ______________________ __________________.

6. Underwater archaeology allows us to maximize the information contained within historic wrecks. By adhering to archaeological methods we can learn much about ancient __________________ ______________________________ and even the lifestyles of the ____.

7. Artifact collection is strictly controlled, just as the collection of corals or other marine life is, and is against the law in every state in the U.S. ____.

8. Being a certified wreck diver does not ______________________ ______________________, it only gives you the license to begin to ____ __________________ that wreck diving offers.

Appendix

Suggested Wreck Diving Equipment Checklist

- ☐ Mask
- ☐ Snorkel & Keeper
- ☐ Fins
- ☐ Exposure Suit
- ☐ Boots
- ☐ Gloves/Mitts
- ☐ Hood
- ☐ Weight System
- ☐ Weights
- ☐ Buoyancy Compensator
- ☐ Cylinder(s) Full
- ☐ Regulator(s)
- ☐ Alternate Air Source(s)
- ☐ Pressure Gauge(s)
- ☐ Watch or Timer(s)
- ☐ Depth Gauge(s)
- ☐ Compass(es)
- ☐ Knives
- ☐ Whistle
- ☐ Dive Computer
- ☐ Defogging Solution
- ☐ Dive Lights/Batteries
- ☐ Chemical Light/ Cylinder Light
- ☐ Tether Line Reel
- ☐ Up-Line Reel
- ☐ Safety Lines for Boat
- ☐ Dive Tables
- ☐ Log Book
- ☐ Certification Card
- ☐ Dive Flag
- ☐ Speargun/Extra Points
- ☐ Goodie Bag
- ☐ Fishing License
- ☐ U/W Camera
- ☐ Flash or Strobe
- ☐ Batteries
- ☐ Film
- ☐ Slate and Pencil
- ☐ Spare Parts Kit
- ☐ Swim Suit
- ☐ Towels
- ☐ Suntan Lotion/Sunscreen
- ☐ First Aid Kit
- ☐ Money for Emergency Calls
- ☐ Money for Air Fills
- ☐ Money for Galley & Tips
- ☐ Passport
- ☐ ______________________
- ☐ ______________________
- ☐ ______________________

A.C.U.A. Site Form

Taken From Wisconsin Field Form

- Name, Address, Phone (best time to contact)
- Popular/Local Name of Site:
- Vessel Type: (schooner, steamer, barge, submarine, etc.)
- Hull Material: (wood, iron, steel, composite, fiberglass, ferro-cement)
- Propulsion: (sail, steam, screw, towed, etc.)
  - — If Sail Powered, Number of Masts:
  - — If Engine Driven, Number of Propeller Blades:
- Site Length:
- Site Width:
- Site Location: (Use any one or all of the following methods of location)
  - — Loran Coordinates:
  - — Latitude/Longitude:
  - — State Plane:
  - — Triangulation From Shore:

    Landmark #1:

    Landmark #2:

    Landmark #3:
- Environment:
  - — Depth:
  - — Bottom Type:
  - — Visibility: (blackout, poor, excellent, etc.)
- Possible Penetration: Yes or No
- Possible Disturbance: Yes or No
- Describe in Own Words What the Site Looks Like: (intact, scattered visible structure, rigging, machinery, cargo, etc.)
- Sketch Site: (include direction and noteworthy bottom features)
- Archival References:

For further information contact your appropriate state/provincial agency.

Index

Student Answer Sheet Directions

- Transfer your study guide answers to the following four Answer Sheet pages.
- Remember to write your name and the date on each page.
- Sign each page after you have reviewed each incorrect answer with your instructor.
- Your instructor will collect these pages during your Wreck Diving program.

STUDENT ANSWER SHEET

STUDENT NAME ____________ PART # ______ DATE ______

Reviewed and Corrected by Student and Instructor:

STUDENT SIGNATURE ____________ INSTRUCTOR SIGNATURE ____________

1. ______________________________
2. ______________________________
3. ______________________________
4. ______________________________
5. ______________________________
6. ______________________________
7. ______________________________
8. ______________________________
9. ______________________________
10. ______________________________
11. ______________________________
12. ______________________________
13. ______________________________
14. ______________________________
15. ______________________________
16. ______________________________
17. ______________________________
18. ______________________________
19. ______________________________
20. ______________________________

STUDENT ANSWER SHEET

STUDENT NAME ______ PART # ______ DATE ______

Reviewed and Corrected by Student and Instructor:

STUDENT SIGNATURE ______ INSTRUCTOR SIGNATURE ______

1. ______
2. ______
3. ______
4. ______
5. ______
6. ______
7. ______
8. ______
9. ______
10. ______
11. ______
12. ______
13. ______
14. ______
15. ______
16. ______
17. ______
18. ______
19. ______
20. ______

STUDENT ANSWER SHEET

STUDENT NAME ____________ PART # ________ DATE ____________

Reviewed and Corrected by Student and Instructor:

STUDENT SIGNATURE ____________ INSTRUCTOR SIGNATURE ____________

1. ____________
2. ____________
3. ____________
4. ____________
5. ____________
6. ____________
7. ____________
8. ____________
9. ____________
10. ____________
11. ____________
12. ____________
13. ____________
14. ____________
15. ____________
16. ____________
17. ____________
18. ____________
19. ____________
20. ____________

STUDENT ANSWER SHEET

STUDENT NAME ______ PART # ______ DATE ______

Reviewed and Corrected by Student and Instructor:

STUDENT SIGNATURE ______ INSTRUCTOR SIGNATURE ______

1. ______
2. ______
3. ______
4. ______
5. ______
6. ______
7. ______
8. ______
9. ______
10. ______
11. ______
12. ______
13. ______
14. ______
15. ______
16. ______
17. ______
18. ______
19. ______
20. ______

STUDENT ANSWER SHEET

STUDENT NAME ______ PART # ______ DATE ______

Reviewed and Corrected by Student and Instructor:

STUDENT SIGNATURE ______ INSTRUCTOR SIGNATURE ______

1. ______
2. ______
3. ______
4. ______
5. ______
6. ______
7. ______
8. ______
9. ______
10. ______
11. ______
12. ______
13. ______
14. ______
15. ______
16. ______
17. ______
18. ______
19. ______
20. ______